FRANK LLOYD WRIGHT'S CHICAGO

FRANK LLOYD WRIGHT'S CHICAGO

THOMAS J. O'GORMAN

THUNDER BAY
P·R·E·S·S

San Diego, California

Thunder Bay Press
An imprint of the Advantage Publishers Group
5880 Oberlin Drive, San Diego, CA 92121-4794
www.thunderbaybooks.com

Produced by PRC Publishing Limited
The Chrysalis Building
Bramley Road, London W10 6SP, United Kingdom

An imprint of **Chrysalis** Books Group

© 2004 PRC Publishing Limited.

Library of Congress Cataloging-in-Publication Data

O'Gorman, Thomas J.
    Frank Lloyd Wright's Chicago / Thomas J. O'Gorman.
      p. cm.
    Includes index.
    ISBN 1-59223-127-6
    1. Wright, Frank Lloyd, 1867–1959--Criticism and interpretation. 2. Prairie school
(Architecture)--Illinois--Chicago Region. 3. Usonian houses--Illinois--Chicago
Region. 4. Architecture--Illinois--Chicago Region. I. Title.

NA737.W7046 2004
720'.92--dc22

                                        2004047937

Printed and bound in China

Picture credits:
Arcaid 323, 406; Corbis/© Bettmann 17, 31, 32, 111, 261, 263,
345, 346, 347, 353, 384; Corbis/ © Farrell Grehan 20; Corbis/
© Underwood & Underwood 9.

The publisher wishes to thank Simon Clay for taking
all other photographs in this book.

1 2 3 4 5 08 07 06 05 04

FOR EMMETT JOSEPH BURKE

"All things once are things forever, Soul, once living, lives forever."

Many people helped in the process of producing this book. Their help was
always gracious, generous and, often, a stimulant to the writer's intellect. The
beauty of this book rests in the exquisite images that the photo genius of Simon
Clay brought about. Working with him on this, our third collaboration,
deepened my eye for the genius of Frank Lloyd Wright. I am grateful for his art
and friendship.

Thank you also goes to the following: the Honorable Edward M. and Honorable
Anne M. Burke, Heidi Sperry and the Chicago Landmarks Commission, David
and Jane Barclay, Derek Gurski, Steve and Monika Hall, Terry and Eve McBride,
John Peterson, Patrick and Penny Fahey, Mr. and Mrs. Meyer Rudoff, David and
Debra Nemeth, John and Mary Brennan, Mr. and Mrs. Donald C. Clark, Mr. and
Mrs. Robert C. Muirhead and family, Frank Lucente, Kurt Gustafson, Steven C.
Bern, John Major, Jane Graham, Peggy Bently, John Noitz, James Campbell,
Marcia Tharp, Bill Muller, Mrs. Hurley Teague, Walter Sobol, Bruce Haines, John
Dale Tilton, Mr. and Mrs. J. Alwatter, Mrs. George Sample, Dr. and Mrs. Kevin J.
O'Donoghue, Theodore Smith, Mr. and Mrs. Edward S. Busche, Richard Talaske,
Mr. and Mrs. Mark P. Donovan, Mr. and Mrs. Edward Behringer, Mr. and Mrs.
James Farrell, Revival Inc., Mark Steinke, Lindy Fleming, the Newberry Library,
the Daniel Burnham Library of the Art Institute of Chicago, the Harold
Washington Library, Mark and Mary Beth Bowman, and Martin Dolan.

CONTENTS

INTRODUCTION

When Frank Lloyd Wright created his world-famous architectural design center in Spring Green, Wisconsin, amid the rolling countryside to which his immigrant grandparents first came, he named the center "Taliesin." The name, meaning literally "the shining brow," was from the Welsh bard who sang the praises of art and architecture at the court of King Arthur. Taliesin was a gentle prophet of Celtic myth who told the story of the shape-shifter with the power to take on all forms; an appropriate metaphor for Frank Lloyd Wright, the artist and architect whose lifelong career reinvented the shape of American tastes and American homes.

Frank Lloyd Wright embodied the character of America with his remarkable architectural designs. His great, long life (1867–1959) and the ongoing evolution of modern technology allowed him to reinvent both himself and his aesthetic sense of American design over and over again. For him, architecture was "the great final proof of quality in any civilization whatsoever." That is Wright's way of saying that the transparency of architecture reveals the deepest characteristics of any culture. What we build and how we build express who we are and what we value. Do we create for beauty, practicality, or necessity? Throughout his almost one hundred years of living, Wright's career found him designing structures that were to be expressive of all such rationales.

It was perhaps Wright's sense of place, more than any other factor, that made his life's work so dramatically American, Midwestern, and Prairie-centered. He designed from the soil from which he came, the rolling midlands of the nation's interior, rich and textured, filled with the spirit of the pioneer and evocative of the power that drove Americans from sea to sea in the decades following the Civil War. As Americans spread out across the continent for which they struggled, they literally built a nation in the wilderness. The era of Wright's life corresponds to the most dramatic period of American settlement in our history. It is a period that witnessed the birth and the massive growth and redevelopment of American cities and its suburbs. The sleepy suburban Arts and Crafts country villages of Wright's early career, in which his Prairie-style homes thrived over the course of half a century, were transformed into the new homes of the nation's burgeoning middle class. Suburban populations exploded, growing beyond all proportions during Wright's final years from the postwar baby boom. While necessity redesigned aesthetics, Wright endeavored to marry together both of these concepts in his radically new American synthesis, the modernist Usonian style.

Right: A photograph taken in 1930 of Frank Lloyd Wright in New York next to an architectural model of his work.

8

Remarkably, both styles for which Wright became so well-known, Prairie and Usonian, served as the bookends of the architect's career. Nowhere is that better expressed or visibly seen than in Chicago and its surrounding suburbs. Wright's earliest works made their debut in Chicago, the most rapidly growing big city in America in the last decades of the nineteenth century and the first decades of the twentieth. The journey to Chicago as an eager young man of vision and talent became the making of Frank Lloyd Wright, as it was for many of his generation. In Chicago, Wright discovered the nation's most intriguing and inventive architects and an urban population with the sophistication to reward bold architectural design. In Chicago, Wright shared his inventiveness with men like Joseph Silsbee, Louis Sullivan, Dankmar Adler, and Daniel Burnham in the years just prior to the World's Columbian Exposition of 1893. At the World's Fair, almost exclusively designed by Burnham in the neoclassical style, twenty-seven million visitors came to see what was heralded as the approaching age of the modern. Wright was at Louis Sullivan's side drawing the design that Sullivan created for the famed Transportation Building, the most significant non-neoclassical structure of the exposition. Architecture, then, was truly the coin of the realm in Chicago and as daring as Wright presented himself, he was to discover clients of equal daring, eager for his fresh inventiveness and radical designs.

The houses and structures that are cataloged in this book take the reader into the vision and dream that was within Frank Lloyd Wright at the beginning of his career in Chicago, expanding over the next half century throughout the surrounding region. Eighteen of Wright's Chicago designs still stand and flourish in contemporary use. Families still live their lives in his unique dwellings, conserving, restoring, and protecting his legacy. Twenty-four of his designs for domestic residences have almost developed the status of sacred totems in suburban Oak Park, where he and his family lived for twenty years. Another eight structures in nearby River Forest enrich the landscape, giving it texture with a ghostly beauty that never seems to fade. In addition to these fifty, there are more than another fifty additional dwellings, in less concentrated numbers, in other surrounding communities near Chicago. They represent a unique heritage, a stunning expression of American architectural design, and an impact of historic significance in the heartland of the nation.

Each of Wright's works came about as the result of the architect's collaboration with clients, often people of equal inventiveness and technological understanding. Their names are forever tied to the homes they commissioned, hence the custom of naming each structure to honor the foresight and courage of the first owners. This book is also about them, who they were,

Left: Taliesin clings to the side of the hill in its idyllic setting. The building materials are primarily native limestone, wood, and plaster surfacing, and the complex has seen many alterations over the years.

and how they came to select the irascible Mr. Wright as their architect of choice. Sometimes the partnerships blossomed into lifelong friendships. At other times, clients became the nitro to Wright's glycerin; in situations marked with harsh words and bitter feelings clouding the best-laid plans. But overall, Wright had great appeal to a particular type of savvy, eccentric, well-educated, self-made individual. His clients were not particularly people of tremendous wealth, but rather people of means with tremendous appreciation for the modern innovation that they could see in Wright's works. Coming to understand the architect's appeal to these individuals gives us a further understanding of Wright himself and the genius of his designs.

Each Wright house is a story unto itself. The array of characters, the drama involved in each architectural creation, and the ultimate conclusion of each project all show elements of intriguing humanity and artistic curiosity. In many of Wright's early designs, we can come to recognize elements of enduring importance that the architect used throughout his lifetime of work. We can see in the development of his style an evolution that was always ahead of its time. What is remarkable about the centrality of Chicago to Wright's designs is the exciting process which ultimately gave birth to what Wright came to call his "Prairie" house. This book will give the reader a productive, handy, working knowledge of all the distinctive elements of that Prairie design. After an absence of more than thirty years from the Chicago area, Wright returned just before World War II with a new architectural design expression that was more modern, utilitarian, and economical than his earlier works. Using the acronym "Usonian" (for United States of North America) to describe this new, edgy domestic design, Wright would spend the later years of his life after the war creating extraordinary examples of this style throughout the Chicago area. The reader will also come to a fuller understanding of the details of this critical Wright style through the many examples of Usonian homes that so richly cluster in this region.

Great similarities often link the works of Wright. Their artistic characters come from the same gene pool that is uniquely American. Perhaps that is why Wright was always so appealing. More than any other American architect, his work is readily recognizable as inherently a part of our own culture, our own history, and our own identity as a people. He spent his life eschewing the revivalist styles that copied the designs of historic periods of the past. He had little appreciation for their rehashing of past aesthetics. What Wright always brought to the table was something uniquely American, an artistry that was robust, graceful, inventive, and, most of all, fashioned to fit the lifestyles of his fellow citizens.

To assist the reader in expanding his or her knowledge of Wright's extraordinary designs, photographer Simon Clay has brought a keen eye for photographing the detail and long shots that bring each work to life. Study the

Above: Detail of a memorial at Taliesin East.

horizontal and vertical lines, the roofs, the windows, and the shapes of each building. Look for similarities. Observe differences. See the connections that link Wright's architecture to one another. Test their practicality. Question their utility. Go visit them in person if you have the chance.

There is no denying that Chicago is the capital of the American heartland, a designation that is as much a reflection of its geographical centrality as it is its mercantile and political significance. Such human crafts find a hearty home in Chicago. Architecture, itself, is a human craft, which for Wright was imbued with a unique sense of the organic, which was his way of expressing architecture that arose out of nature itself. Whether a Prairie mansion, a commercial warehouse, a sweepingly modern farmhouse, a daringly imaginative chicken coop, or one of the most resourceful churches in America, Wright's designs echo a simplicity found deep within the very heart of nature. It is a concept that would not have seemed strange to Wright's mystical Celtic forebears at home among the dolmens of the ancient past and the heartland hills of rural Wisconsin. From them, Wright inherited a powerful sense of the primeval landscape, the arcane energy of the earth. In this can be found his intense connection to the heartland landscape of the prairie. This was the geography on which Wright built a new sense of the American home. And it is the passion with which he sang the praises of artistic design from one century to another. Wright's legacy is an artistic adhesive that binds the aesthetics of the heartland to the soul of the nation with refined elegance and innovative utility, two distinctly American graces forged in the genius of the nation's greatest architect.

Left: One of the main thoroughfares of Oak Park, Forest Avenue features a number of fine examples of Wright's early work, including the Harem—the Frank Wright Thomas house—the Heurtley residence, and the forerunner of Fallingwater, the Mrs. Thomas H. Gale House.

FRANK LLOYD WRIGHT'S LIFE 1867–1877

Frank Lloyd Wright was the greatest architect America ever produced. His fresh architectural designs reinvented domestic architecture and changed the way many Americans lived. His houses seemed to rise out of the landscape in which they were created. Even his commercial designs reshaped the utility and sensitivities of corporate tastes. His earliest designs were an assault on the aesthetics of the quietude and predictable tastes of ordinary Americans. He appealed to a remarkable array of savvy, adventurous, self-made men of business who saw in his work the streamlined coming of the modern age. His clients were not the elite of local society. Instead, they were often inventors, tinkerers, and innovators themselves, who recognized in Wright a familiar, companion genius. From his Oak Park home and studio to the Guggenheim Museum on Fifth Avenue in New York, he straddled an effusive era of dramatic change. From the lightbulb to the jet plane, Wright delighted in the inventiveness of the age in which fate had thrust him, conscious that all too often his genius forced him to run ahead of the others, reaching further into the unprecedented possibilities unfolding around him.

When Frank Lloyd Wright was born in 1867, in the rolling countryside of Richland Center, Wisconsin, Andrew Johnson was the seventeenth president of the United States, Abraham Lincoln had been dead only two years, and the greatest conflict in the history of the nation, the war between the states, had ceased with the silence of a shaky peace less than two years before. Remarkably, at the time of Wright's death in 1959 at the age of ninety-two, Dwight Eisenhower was completing his second term as the nation's thirty-fourth president. Wright had enjoyed a significant longevity, bright and facile through the length of his days. Time supplied Wright with an ability to encode an understanding of the age in which he lived. From horseback to fancy motorcars, the beginning and end of Wright's eventful lifespan was galvanized by promise, a family attribute that was as much an inherited gift as it was the product of his curious family's own unique making.

Wright's most important influence, emotionally and spiritually, was his mother's family, the Lloyd Joneses, a group of colorful religious dissenters whose origins were in the Welsh countryside near the village of Llandyssul. It is said that from there the blue stones that fashioned Stonehenge were cut. It is not insignificant that among the ancestors of his family were men who had the stonemason's trade.

Wright's maternal grandparents, Richard Jones and Mary Lloyd, produced seven children in a family that came to be known as the Lloyd Joneses. In 1844, they left Wales, emigrating to the United States and eventually relocating to Spring Green,

Right: An early portrait of a young Frank Lloyd Wright taken around 1926.

16

Wisconsin, the later site of Wright's beloved Taliesin. So many of their Welsh relations joined them in that fertile valley in southern Wisconsin that it appeared to take on the spirit of the land that they had left. Their homestead resembled the traditional thatched Welsh cottage of their earlier life. Wright's grandfather was a farmer and a lay Unitarian preacher. The influence of the Unitarian Church was important and powerful throughout Wright's life. It provided a network of familial and cultural connections. Wright's uncle Jenkins Lloyd Jones became a Unitarian minister and later commissioned Wright's first architectural employer in Chicago, Joseph Silsbee, to design his church, All Souls, in Chicago. Silsbee also designed a small Unitarian chapel in a village near Spring Green in 1886. Wright may have worked on this project with him. Some of Wright's most important later clients were Unitarians, most notably the Coonleys and Charles E. Roberts. The Unity Temple in Oak Park remains one of Wright's most recognizable designs.

Anna Lloyd Jones, Wright's mother, was a bright girl and an even more determined woman. When she met William Cary Wright, the architect's father, she was a schoolteacher seventeen years his junior. He was already married with a family. Following the death of his wife, Wright married Anna in 1866 against the protests of her family who were not enamored with the accomplished forty-one-year-old Amherst- and Yale-educated romantic and jack-of-all-trades who was a minister, lawyer, piano teacher, rhetoric master, and restless dreamer. They would endure a loveless marriage of endless unhappiness, in a house filled with stepchildren who became the victims of Anna Lloyd Wright's anger and frustration.

Frank Lloyd Wright was born in 1867, one year after his parents' marriage, and is said to have inherited both his father's sense of practical order and his ungrounded sense of tragic restlessness. Family members saw him absorb his mother's sense of the love of beauty and aesthetic intuition. Anna Lloyd Wright spent the remainder of her life obsessed with the comings and goings of her son. Wright, in his autobiographical writings, describes the exaggerated sense of devotion between mother and son. There is no denying that the energized spirit with which Wright shaped his architectural career owed much to both parents. But it is also true that from each he inherited a wildly dysfunctional personality and a skewed sense of his own importance, even in childhood. Despite the idyllic picture Wright paints of his early years—prophetic announcements by his pregnant mother that she had conceived an architect, and a childhood thick with art and literature to nourish his future genius—the reality of the tragic human events in the architect's personal life are a sad commentary on it. William Cary Wright was long estranged and physically absent from his family. In 1884, after eighteen years of unhappiness, he filed for divorce from Anna on the grounds she had abandoned him and their marriage bed. He died in 1904, on the eve of his eightieth birthday. Frank Lloyd Wright did not attend his father's funeral. Nor did he attend his mother's in 1923.

Left: Frank Lloyd Wright's home and studio in Oak Park gave the architect a chance to fully express his vision, and the building is a monument to form, structure, and ornamentation.

FRANK LLOYD WRIGHT'S LIFE
1878–1887

Below: A view of Taliesin, designed by Wright in Spring Green, Wisconsin. It is named for a Welsh bard of mythical stature.

Below: Wright was a complete designer and even the smallest detail did not escape him. His typeface—Eaglefeather—is always associated with him. This memorial at Taliesin East gives a birth date of 1869; he was in fact born in 1867.

Wright's childhood and adolescence were shadowed by geographic upheaval, the result of his father's nomadic movements with his family to positions at Baptist churches in New England—first in Pawtucket, Rhode Island, and later, Weymouth, Massachusetts. These postings to faraway places intensified Anna Lloyd Wright's emotional instability and expanded the family's overall deepening unhappiness. An unusual move by

William Cary Wright, changing his Baptist affiliation to Unitarian, in 1878, was certainly an homage to the Lloyd Joneses and may have even been an attempt to establish some stability within Wright's blended family. This religious transition was further enhanced by the return of the Wrights to Wisconsin with the purchase of a house in Madison along the waters of Lake Mendota. If William Cary Wright was ever a popular man among his in-laws, it was at the time of this move. Within easy reach of the familiar hills of Spring Green, it was also the start of the tradition of young Frank spending his summers with his mother's family on the farm of his Uncle James. Although the young Frank recognized his dislike for the smelly, messy chores of farm and barnyard, this period made him aware of the importance of the nearness of nature in all its organic richness to the places and events of everyday life. Wright experienced the tactile wonders of nature firsthand. Their significance would last for the rest of his life.

Few can dispute the high genius of Frank Lloyd Wright. His ability to think in multiple dimensions would be the great secret of his professional success. He could envision an architectural structure in all its complexity and then take pencil to paper, laying out every minute detail in every conceivable perspective of proportion. Incredibly, however, he never graduated from high school or college. Certainly no barrier to anyone's successful future in the late nineteenth century, the absence of formal education in him is made more ironic because education was a Lloyd Jones family industry. That their most cherished Frank found formal education difficult might be a further expression of his genius. But, he would always feel the social stigma resulting from his eccentric inability to do well in institutional education settings. A brief stint at the engineering school of the University of Wisconsin in Madison is all he could muster in his higher education. In later life, Wright would often expand on the truth, admitting falsely that he had a longer academic career there than he actually experienced.

So, nourished by the eccentricities of an extended family of wildly independent thinkers, indulged and annoyed by a mother of cloyingly intensive emotional control, watchful of the disintegration of his own family's domestic happiness, conscious of his own intellectual giftedness and academic carelessness, and armed with an outrageous sense of his own individual entitlement, Frank Lloyd Wright abandoned his life in Wisconsin for the drama of Chicago at the age of twenty. While he would later boast of his spirit of independence and self-motivation in the move to the big thriving metropolis to the south, any scrutiny of his courageousness must be tempered by the influence cast by his Unitarian minister uncle, the Reverend Jenkins Lloyd Jones. Though Wright spent his life relishing the tale that he found his first architectural job in Chicago through his own resources, it is suspicious that his first employer, Joseph Lyman Silsbee, was an architect with close ties to his uncle. In fact, Silsbee had already designed a Unitarian church for his uncle in Spring Green the previous year, 1886. Wright was not quite the unknown commodity he liked others to believe.

1889

 ## FRANK LLOYD WRIGHT HOME AND STUDIO

Address: 428 Forest Avenue, Oak Park, Illinois

Date: 1889. Playroom and dining room additions (1895) and studio (1898); the oldest standing house designed by Wright

Work on the brick and shingle residence began in 1889, soon after Wright's marriage to Catherine Tobin, his first wife, whom he was to abandon some twenty years later. To finance the construction of this house, he talked his boss, architect Louis Sullivan, into a five-year contract. He then asked Sullivan to lend him the funds to complete the house, borrowed against

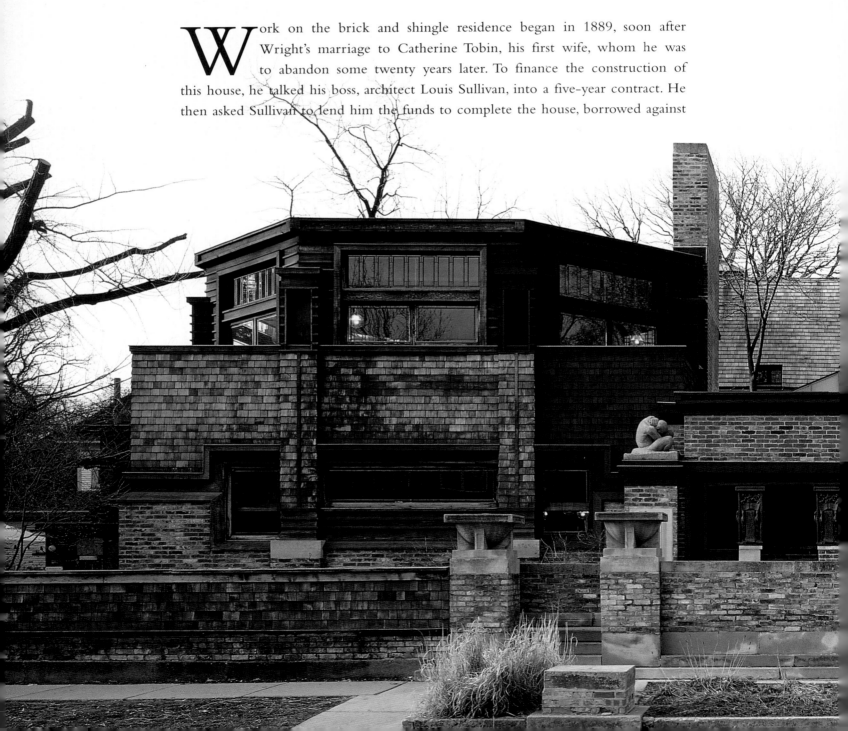

1889

Left: The stork plaque at the entrance to the studio was sculpted by Richard Bock from Wright's detailed drawings.

Main picture: Wright's studio frontage on Chicago Avenue was crucial in establishing the young architect's credentials, and provided an important presence in the burgeoning and progressive suburb of Oak Park.

Below: Detail of exterior sculptures flanking the frontage to Wright's studio.

his five-year deal. This house, with a sweepingly steep roofline, became his architectural headquarters during the remarkable period of profitable productivity in which he designed his well-known Oak Park homes. The house itself reflects the heavy influence of the Arts and Crafts movement and its shingled exterior recalls the influence of Chicago architect Joseph Silsbee, his early mentor.

A refined artistry merges a residential grandeur with the additional utility of a home office that today is enjoying a renewed fashion. There was no separation for Wright here between home life and architecture. When Sullivan fired him for designing "bootlegged" houses on the side, in 1893, this would become the heart of Wright's professional career. Out of here, some of his most remarkable early designs emerged. The Prairie-style house would have its birth and development from here. An addition containing a two-story polygonal bay was completed in 1895 on the south side of the house, giving the enlarged Wright family a new dining room on the

Below: The dining room is made intimate by his cozy scale and proportion and the inclusion of expansive natural lighting. His furniture reflects the handcrafted ethos of the structure.

Right: The barrel-vaulted playroom is fifteen feet high and provides the first dramatic space of Wright's career. The windows are at the height of a child and the overmantel mural took its theme from *The Arabian Nights*.

first floor and an expanded bedroom on the second floor. He also built a two-story structure at the rear of the house that provided a new kitchen and quarters for a maid. Above this, the Wright children received a barrel-vaulted playroom surrounded by rich art-glass windows, as well as a skylight covered in a fret-sawed wooden screen.

In the beginning, Wright had no separate, self-contained architectural studio. Instead, for some eleven years, he used a second-floor room at the front of the house for his drafting room. In 1898, a separate two-story structure was completed at the north end of the house along Chicago Avenue to serve as Wright's office. It has a square first floor of bricks and shingles topped by a horizontal board-and-batten octagonal second floor. The structure includes an octagonal library and a two-story drafting room. A pitched interior ceiling rises twenty-seven feet and contains a suspended encircling balcony held with chains from the roof beams. Wright's office itself was placed behind the reception area with a low-pitched octagonal skylight roof. Outside, brick piers frame the entrance of the studio. As much as this was a home for the Wright family and an office for Wright himself, within the context of the architect's career, it is really the laboratory out of which the Prairie style was born. Devotees of Wright treat the space as sacred ground, carrying the memory of Wright with a peculiar aura and treating his designs like totems.

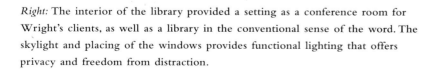

Right: The interior of the library provided a setting as a conference room for Wright's clients, as well as a library in the conventional sense of the word. The skylight and placing of the windows provides functional lighting that offers privacy and freedom from distraction.

FRANK LLOYD WRIGHT'S LIFE 1887–1889

rank Lloyd Wright set out to reinvent the world. Chicago was just the right place to do that. Sixteen years earlier, in 1871, 60 percent of the central business district was leveled by the dramatic winds of a fire that was without equal. In the aftermath, the city built a new urban commercial center that would become the envy of the nation. Chicago was consumed with the detail and minutiae of architecture. Over the course of the previous decade, architects came in large numbers to the city, reflecting the imperative for buildings of substance and innovation. Rarely did a metropolis have the opportunity to erase the shoddy structures of its early years and replace them with buildings more emblematic of its later prominence. Chicago was relishing the enormity of the task that creating a new, modern city was bringing about. It was the place to be. Jobs for skilled workers were there for the taking. At the time of the Great Fire, 300,000 people lived in Chicago. By 1880, the population had grown to half a million. By 1890, there would be more than a million. Growth was explosive. So too were creative ideas that were transforming the city into the capital of the American heartland. Established as a city only in 1837, its location at the juncture of the Chicago River and Lake Michigan provided it with the most important geography in America—at the confluence of the nation's waterways. Thanks to the 1848 engineering phenomenon of the Illinois & Michigan Canal, connecting the Illinois River to the Great Lakes, it was possible to traverse all the inland waterways of the country and arrive in Chicago. The impact this placed on commerce and agricultural trade was profound. The robust economy that resulted permitted Chicago to survive the destruction of the fire. By 1885, two years before the arrival of Wright, architect William LeBaron Jenny built the first skyscraper, the ten-story Home Insurance Building, with the first load-carrying structural frame. Urban life was undergoing a revolution, changing the way people lived and worked. It was an environment tailor-made for Wright.

Wright was only twenty years of age when he arrived on the teeming streets of Chicago. He beat the pavement from one architectural firm to another, attempting to find employment. On the fourth day, supposedly surviving on a banana a day, he took himself to the firm of Joseph Lyman Silsbee, who at that very moment was designing a Chicago church for his uncle on the city's South Side. Wright insists that he had an interview with him without revealing his family connection, showing him sketches he had drawn. But it is almost inconceivable that Silsbee did not know Wright, having most likely collaborated with the young man on the designs for the Unitarian Chapel built near Spring Green in 1886. Silsbee went on to hire Wright as an apprentice. Among his first projects was Silsbee's design for the Hillside Home School near

Right: A young Louis Henry Sullivan, Wright's mentor, poses beside a tree in 1924.

Spring Green, run by Wright's two aunts. While at the firm, Wright would have had ample opportunity to study Silsbee's popular designs for domestic residences—large, sprawling, shingle-sided Queen Anne homes. They were the rage of the day, an architectural style from the historic past. For Wright, such vestiges of history held little interest. Larger, fresher interests grasped his imagination.

Within a year of his arrival, Wright was ready to leave Silsbee's employment. He had a more dramatic goal in mind, the architectural firm of Dankmar Adler and Louis Sullivan. His remarkable skill as a draftsman almost guaranteed his success in being hired. Adler and Sullivan were remarkable men. Adler, the innovative engineer, supervised the most significant of technological elements of their designs. Sullivan, the genius of architectural design, was the artist. He would become Wright's teacher, mentor, and friend. Among the projects Wright worked on was the eighteen-story, mixed-use Auditorium Theater Building, Chicago's tallest building and most sensational wonder of design at its opening in 1890. Wright absorbed the ethos of Sullivan's architectural style, an organic lyricism that found its expression in nature itself. His work was exciting, challenging, and modern. It was said that Wright became the pencil in Sullivan's hand.

Left: A typical street scene of Chicago in 1890, the time that a young Wright would have arrived to start his new career.

1891

 JAMES CHARNLEY HOUSE

Address: 1365 N. Astor Street, Chicago, Illinois
Built: 1891

Late Sullivan and early Wright, this house was designed for Chicago lumber magnate James Charnley, a close friend of Louis Sullivan. Built along one of the city's most refined urban streetscapes, it is the product of Wright's collaboration with his mentor. While working for Sullivan, Wright designed some half-dozen domestic residences between 1888 and 1892. He often did such work at home, during the evenings and on Sundays. But this is by far the most significant of his designs. Here, Wright claims to have "first sensed the decorative value of the plain surface—that is to say—of the flat plane as such." The single openings in the center of plain wall-masses bear this out.

A stately, urbane townhouse, Charnley House stands as a mini Italian palace within just a few hundred yards of the Lake Michigan shoreline and only two blocks south of the verdant edge of Lincoln Park. Despite its cityscape location, nature, in all its array, stands generously nearby. No one in Chicago had ever seen anything like this before. Its exterior is made of golden wheat-colored Roman bricks, those narrow building blocks that so characterize Wright's later Prairie style. The sweep of the façade is broadly horizontal and this sight line is accentuated by the stone banding that is drawn around the structure just below the third floor and above the colonnaded porch above the limestone entryway. This balcony is the structure's most well-known design feature and exudes the Sullivanesque floral filigree so familiar to

Left: The flat rooflines with decorative edging and the filigreed copper balcony façade are emblematic of the Sullivan-Wright artistry.

Right: The Astor Street façade of the Charnley-Persky House is augmented by Roman brick and limestone. The copper-columned balcony is dramatically horizontal and reflects the stunning, brief combination of Wright and his mentor, Louis Sullivan.

Chicagoans from his many other important city designs, among which is the Carson Pirie Scott Department Store on South State Street. Amber art glass and a great wooden door set with lush floral metalwork mark the entryway set in limestone. Generous chimneys, also of Roman brick, sit at the north and south ends of the house. Eight square windows set in groups of four provide light to the basement area while establishing the façade with further geometric balance. Similar windows, scaled smaller and set in pairs, are aligned across the fourth story of the house, further providing a graceful tapering. A protruding cornice-overhang provides an architectural polish that Wright would later further extend as one of his signature design elements in future structures.

For many years Wright received little credit for his contributions to this important domestic residence. He had previously designed a beach house for Charnley in 1890 in Ocean Springs, Mississippi. Wright and Sullivan would part company soon after the completion of Charnley House. The Chicago architectural firm of Skidmore, Owings, and Merrill, creators of such modern classic Chicago buildings as the Inland Steel Building, the John Hancock Center, and the Sears Tower, purchased Charnley House in 1986. They carried out a restoration in 1988 under architect John Eifler. Subsequently, the building was purchased by Chicago developer and architectural historian Seymour H. Persky. He gifted it to the Society of Architectural Historians as their headquarters, and the name officially became the Charnley-Persky House.

Above: Louis Sullivan's signature floral carvings in rich oak are emblematic of the interior style of the Charnley-Persky House and future Wright artistry.

Left: The interior of the Charnley-Persky House shimmers in rich woods from the great natural light supplied by skylights. This interior shape is reminiscent of the form Wright later used in the famed Larkin Building in Buffalo, New York.

1892

THOMAS H. GALE HOUSE

Address: 1027 Chicago Avenue, Oak Park, Illinois
Built: 1892

This handsome Queen Anne–style house that so mirrors its nearby neighbor, the Robert P. Parker House, is architecturally descended from the design of the Robert Emmond House, also 1892, in LaGrange, Illinois, just southwest of Oak Park. All three houses are "bootlegged" homes, referring to Wright's sideline business practice of designing homes while in the employment of Chicago architects Dankmar Adler and Louis Sullivan. Thomas Gale, the real estate

investor who lived in this house, built it and its neighbor on speculation. The home is designed in the rectilinear format. Large, sloping, high-pitched, shingled roof designs like this are emblematic of this early period of Wright homes. So too are the polygonal dormers that add so much character to his domestic design. Once again, Wright owes a debt to his first teacher, Joseph Silsbee, whose Queen Anne artistry first engaged Wright, as well as to Louis Sullivan, from whom he learned the art of simplifying the geometric massing of the rooflines. Large octagonal bays rise on both the first and second front floors, but here the exciting design feature is the east side of the house, with its many windows adding distinction and grandeur to the overall design of the house. The high, sweeping, hipped roof further gives extended angularity and shape to the house. To Wright, this house and its neighbor were small dwellings with inexpensive details, but they continue to tell us much about the artistry that is so abundant in Wright's work. Its simple front entrance, iron rails, and stairs distinguish it from its neighbor.

Above: A side view of the Gale House displays Wright's use of multiple sets of windows, framed in the Prairie style, to fill the interior with as much natural light as possible.

Right: Wright's earliest structures were expressions of historic revival styles. Here, he designed a popular Queen Anne–style home, bootlegged while working for Sullivan and Adler.

ROBERT P. PARKER HOUSE

Address: 1019 Chicago Avenue, Oak Park, Illinois

Date: 1892

Thomas Gale sold this two-story turreted bay house, just two doors west of his own home, to Robert Parker, a lawyer. The exterior of the house differs from the Thomas Gale House by the entranceway that reflects a restoration carried out in the 1990s. The rich exterior color motif—deep, muted red, almost cinnabar—and dark chocolate-brown trim accentuates the fine Prairie-style windows and overall shape of the house. The height of the robust bay has more verticality in this color treatment and permits much of the Wrightian detail to be appreciated. The windows on the second floor have more grace and actual length than at the Thomas Gale House. This is Queen Anne elegance at its best. Horizontal cladding accentuates the flow of the exterior lines.

Above: The two-story turreted bay is enhanced by Wright's simple Prairie-style windows that give the revivalist house its own peculiar modernity.

Wright imbued the Parker House with the symmetry and proportion that he used throughout his career to create designs of perfect aesthetical balance. His soaring roofs, here, give great verticality, while his exterior cladding provides complementary horizontal character.

Above: The Emmond House is among Wright's earliest designs and has a strong similarity to the Thomas Gale and Robert Parker houses in Oak Park. The Emmond House's twin octagonal towers and handsome roofline are expressive of Wright's harmonious aesthetic.

ROBERT G. EMMOND HOUSE

Address: 109 South Eighth
Avenue, LaGrange, Illinois
Built: 1892

This leafy western suburban community was the perfect setting for Wright's rambling Queen Anne-style residence for Robert G. Emmond. This is by far a more expansive structure than the Thomas Gale House or the Robert Parker House, Emmond's similar Oak Park mates. Wright designed this house while working for Adler and Sullivan, a fact that permits this house to have the "moonlighted" pedigree. Though following a similar rectilinear plan, the further addition by Wright of a second eight-sided two-story bay adds a more elaborate mass to the corners of the house, and the steep octagonal roofs give each the character of a tower. The octagonal format gives shape to both the home's dining room and the living room. The lower exterior of the structure was reclad in brick in the mid-1930s with a further expansion and enclosing of the terrace. Horizontal cladding rises on the second stories of the bays that are plumb with the low eave overhangs. Dormer windows, with their own deep overhangs, are in the steep sweep of the main roof. Together these angular shapes and geometric roof treatments give the house powerful character across the rooflines. Peter Groan, the father of Emmond's long-time friend Orrin Groan of the National Biscuit Company, would later build his own Frank Lloyd Wright home on the opposite side of Eighth Avenue.

IRVING CLARK HOUSE

Address: 211 S. LaGrange Road, LaGrange, Illinois
Date: 1892

Plans for this house were only discovered in the 1960s at Taliesin, ascribing the design to Wright. For many years it was thought to be the work of architect E. Hill Turnock. This is Wright's earliest bootlegged house in LaGrange and represents an evolution in his design method. The exterior echoes Wright's own Oak Park residence with emphasis on the powerful front gable with a cross gable (the main peak is bisected by a perpendicular peak across the central axis of the house) and the entryway placed between two octagonal bays. Dormers protrude with a similar A-framed roof design on each side of the house. The effect is a small mountain range of rooftop peaks that express an intense sense of being sheltered, an overriding theme within the Prairie motif that Wright was to expand upon.

Those familiar with the house Wright designed for Judge S. A. Foster in West Pullman, on Chicago's South Side, can see the pattern of a similar steep, chaletlike shadow in the deep A-frames of the roofs. The tall brick chimney that rises above the roofline is both practical and aesthetic, becoming a familiar Wright design theme. A second chimney, wider and lower, sits atop the center of the house. It was used again in the George W. Smith House in Oak Park in 1896 with equal effectiveness. He employed his own version of Palladian windows, with a modern crispness, on the second floor façade, above the home's twin entry bays. The soaring design of the roof pitch is further emphasized by the single front third-story "Chicago" three-sided window topped by a half-moon-shaped window, known as a "lunette." Wright's rounded inset brick doorframes have a familiar Sullivanesque quality to them and design-thread that leads to that upper rounded lunette window. The front porch is open without any exterior enclosure. But the house has ample entryways, with guests entering at the front, servants at the rear, and family through a side door on the north side of the house, giving access to transportation, while a south-side entry gives passage to the side yard. The house also has a side porch on the south. The exterior skin of the house is horizontal board-and-batten.

Right: A detail from one of the Wright-designed windows.

Above: The tall brick chimneys that rise above the roofline are a familiar Wright design theme.

GEORGE BLOSSOM HOUSE

Address: 4858 S. Kenwood Avenue, Chicago, Illinois
Built: 1892

The Kenwood community is a Chicago neighborhood with long-standing patrician elegance. It was once known as "the Lake Forest of the South Side," a reference to Chicago's North Shore, lakefront suburb of old money and landed gentry. The Kenwood neighborhood was home to the true barons of Chicago industry, men like steel magnate and *Titanic* victim Martin Ryerson, meatpacker Gustavus Swift, and Sears Roebuck executive Julius Rosenwald. In its heyday, these powerbrokers filled the neighborhood with homes by architects such as Benjamin Marshall, George Maher, and Howard Van Doren Shaw. It was elite geography, one that held great appeal for Wright. Kenwood was also the neighborhood in which Catherine Tobin, the first Mrs. Wright, lived when she and the architect were first dating. Wright recalls in his autobiography the times he and Catherine walked hand in hand "like children" through the neighborhood, observing the expansion of neighborhood mansions. But despite decades on the downside in modern times, this neighborhood has been revitalized now by new money and well-educated homeowners who relish its easy access to downtown Chicago and the intellectual ambience of its neighbor, the famed University of Chicago. Streets are thick here with restored mansions of quality and revitalized historic homes.

Wright designed this house for George Blossom, a successful Chicago businessman, in the American Colonial Revival style. Such historical architecture will seem out of place for those familiar with Wright's various later signature modern styles. This is one of the last such houses Wright designed in a revival motif. Despite the familiar earmarks of the eighteenth-century-style, a symmetrical façade, Ionic columns, spacious rounded veranda, balustrade along the second-floor balcony, horizontal cladding, Doric pilasters, a form of Palladian window, the handsome hipped roof, wide, overhanging eaves, and the narrowness of the cladding permits a touch of the emerging Wright to show through. He managed to imbue the house with a sense of horizontal sweep that has a distinctive modern quality to it, as well as a sense of what is yet to come from him. The narrow horizontal cladding is expressly American Colonial, reminiscent of outstanding wood-clad houses in New England such as the Lady Pepperell House in New Hampshire and the King Hooper House in Marblehead, Massachusetts. The Blossom House is also one of Wright's bootlegged houses, designed while he was still working for the Chicago firm of Adler and Sullivan. Fifteen years later, in 1907, Wright would design a two-story carriage house for Blossom that was unmistakably executed in the Prairie style.

Left: Despite the American Colonial revival style of the Blossom House, Wright's hand is easily seen in the graceful flow of its hipped roof and in the generous projections of the overhangs, elements that define his later Prairie style.

Above: This art-glass entryway window with intricate metal caming, or leading, permits much natural light into the interior of the Blossom House.

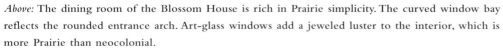

Above: The dining room of the Blossom House is rich in Prairie simplicity. The curved window bay reflects the rounded entrance arch. Art-glass windows add a jeweled luster to the interior, which is more Prairie than neocolonial.

Above: The barrel-vault entryway frames the living room of the Blossom House. The central hearth features a Prairie inglenook with built-in seats. Wright believed his own furniture best fitted the aesthetics of his homes. For him, it was a total package.

Above right: The art-glass windows of the Blossom dining room are effusively simple and geometric, with metal caming fashioning small glass pieces into a pattern that is intrinsically effusive and almost mathematical.

Right: Detail of side window in Blossom House entryway. Geometric forms are fastened with soldered metal.

WARREN MCARTHUR HOUSE

Address: 4852 S. Kenwood Avenue, Chicago, Illinois

Date: 1892

Wright's gambrel-roofed residence for McArthur, a partner in the Ham Lantern Company, reflects the Dutch Colonial revival style that early settlers in America liked because its large-surfaced, double-sloped roof provided them with a large amount of interior attic space. Here, Wright had three dormer windows on the second story rise above the entranceway located on the side of the house, which had been placed to sit perpendicular to the street. Such a shift in its placement permits the expansive girth of the house to be easily seen from the front.

This is another house designed by Wright at the time that he was still working for Adler and Sullivan. Like the Charnley House, he employed narrow, Roman brick across the exterior of the house. Here, it rises up to the first-floor sill beneath the windows. The remainder of the exterior wall above this line is clad in plaster. At each end of the house octagonal bays are cantilevered out from the sides of the structure.

Above: The gambrel roof of the McArthur House is seen in profile as the house sits sideways to the street. Fashioned of narrow, dark, Roman brick, it is among one of Wright's earliest designs.

1893

WALTER M. GALE HOUSE

Address: 1031 Chicago Avenue, Oak Park, Illinois
Date: 1893

This is the last of the three Wright houses to be built along this stretch of Chicago Avenue. It is by far the largest of the Queen Anne–style triplets here. Walter Gale was a prosperous pharmacist, the brother of developer Thomas Gale, who lived next door. This is a variation on the Emmond House and the neighboring Parker and Gale Houses. It is a large house—five bedrooms and three bathrooms that stretch for 4,000 square feet over four floors. Wright was nearing his goal of leaving behind such a historical style of design. The massing of the highly pitched, sweeping, shingled roof has an intense geometry to it. It is enhanced by the recent stripping of the exterior cladding. The natural horizontal wood now expresses more character than its previous cream-paint skin.

The unusually tall, narrow brick chimney at the east end of the roof further refines the geometry of the house and demonstrates a design feature that would become an essential element in all future Wright homes. Large, leaded, diamond-shaped windows add both elegance and lightness to the structure that has a distinctive Ruskin/Arts and Crafts flavor. The square-shaped windows that circle the conical tower heighten the sense of architectural drama, while bringing light into the interior. Dormer windows are particularly high—two stories across the front of the house—and have an intricate carved embellishment. This is Queen Anne style "and then some," a blend of historical style and Wright's passion for innovative purity of purpose. Deep eaves reach a whole new exaggeration that Wright would never abandon. Rich wood intensifies the interior whose beamed ceilings and tiled fireplaces are heralds of future Prairie-style refinements.

Right: The design of the Walter M. Gale House, with its spindle railing and open porch is unique to Wright's early work. Most of the architect's later Prairie houses had porches with roofs.

FRANCIS J. WOOLEY HOUSE

Address: 1030 Superior Street,
Oak Park, Illinois
Built: 1893

A high-pitched, hipped roof framed by multiple dormers with deep overhangs is a central feature of this handsome three-story house built originally for lawyer Francis J. Wooley. Wright later brought Wooley's son, Taylor, into his studio in Oak Park. Polygonal bay windows shape the southeastern portion of the structure. Foundation walls of rough stone are now enhanced, as a restoration of the original horizontal clapboard cladding was recently completed. The entry porch with deep eaves repeats the high-pitched lines of the roof and frames the façade with graceful proportions. The soft, earth tones of the house further enhance this more conventional Wrightian domestic residence that fits easily into the Oak Park landscape, just off historic Forest Avenue. This house sits back to back with its neighbor on Chicago Avenue, the Robert Parker House. The house reflects Wright's passion for designing homes that were affordable. The house is reflective of the nearby Thomas Gale House and continues to echo the style of Wright's first architectural employer, Joseph Silsbee. The strong influence of the Arts and Crafts movement is still embedded in Wright's work at this time. He became an architect of some significance in later years in the Salt Lake City area. This is a comfortable house, one that after more than a century retains the aesthetic of Wright's genius and early designs.

Right: The grandeur of Wright's architectural beginnings is frozen in the Queen Anne splendor of the Wooley House, rich with massive bays and powerful upper-roof projections.

WILLIAM HERMAN WINSLOW HOUSE AND STABLE

Address: 515 Auvergne Place, River Forest, Illinois

Built: 1893

This house is Wright's first and most famous River Forest house, designed when he was only twenty-six years old. It is also his first Prairie house and the connection to the Charnley-Persky House design is apparent. This house also marks Wright's first independent commission after leaving Adler and

Sullivan's firm. It was designed for W. H. Winslow, of the Winslow Ornamental Iron Works, who Wright first knew from his many consulting visits to the offices of Adler and Sullivan. It was Winslow's company that produced Louis Sullivan's famed entryway on the Carson, Pirie, Scott Department Store on Chicago's State Street. In addition to having the distinction of giving Wright his first proper job, an independent commission, Winslow was also the man who later joined Wright in publishing the sermon of Unitarian Minister William Gannett, called *The House Beautiful*, an aesthetic creed urging simple beauty in home design.

Wright brought to the Winslow House many design characteristics that would last throughout his whole career. Among

Below: Wright revolutionized architecture with his design of the Winslow House at the dawn of his career, creating both controversy and the edgiest architecture in America.

these features was the use of deep overhangs, as well as the use of thin, Roman brick on the exterior cladding instead of the more familiar Chicago common brick. This produced proportions with a more graceful horizontal line that soon became emblematic of the Prairie style. He also included ornamental embellishments within the exterior masonry that mirrored Sullivan's organic foliated design motifs. His use of a stylobate foundation, in which the house sat on a cement plane rather than rising out of the more common deeply dug base within the earth, became another common feature of his design from this commission. The aesthetics in use here became an extension of Wright himself.

His use of square windows across the first floor is reminiscent of his employment of them with equal success on the façade of the Charnley-Persky House. So massive are they here, however, that the rectangular front entranceway is dwarfed by their proportionality that is both crisp and modern. Three double-hung rectangular windows balance and shorten the brow line across the first floor. These windows seem to peer above the horizontal banding, or trim band, that runs the width of the house and separates the high first floor from the shorter second floor. The upward sweep of the symmetrical hipped roof and the generous overhang of the roof appear to complete the proportionality of the house's horizontal character. Wright also designed an extraordinary stable for the Winslows that later was converted into a garage, reflecting the graceful lines and proportions of the house. The simplicity of the front façade of the house stands in stark contrast to the rear of the house that reveals a fluid layout oriented around the needs of the family. Wright enclosed the rear porch area sometime after 1894. A dining bay, kitchen facilities, central chimney, and the porch demonstrate the functional side of the house that is fashioned with equal proportion and balance. The Winslow House is an architectural watershed for Wright.

Frank Lloyd Wright explained, "The Winslow House has burst on the view of that provincial suburb like the Prima Vera in full bloom. It was a new world to Oak Park and River Forest. The House became an attraction, far and near. Incessantly it was courted and admired. Ridiculed, too, of course…The first house soon began to shift the sheep from the goats."

After this, his concept of the wall, for instance, was never the same again. Winslow Ornamental Iron Works would later produce the elevator grills for Wright's remodeling of the Rookery Building.

Left: An aerial perspective of the Winslow House provides a clear view of the massive hip roof, the central chimney, and the extraordinary proportions of the house and landscape.

1894

PETER GOAN HOUSE

Address: 108 S. Eighth Avenue, LaGrange, Illinois
Built: 1894

This board-and-batten-looking exterior is really horizontal-patterned shingles, laid to appear to be horizontal battens. They continue up to the sill line of the second floor. This house is considered to be Wright's last bootlegged design while at the firm of Adler and Sullivan. It sits directly across the street from the Emmond House. The subsequent removal of a front porch that spread across the full width of the house has altered the façade, though it succeeds in placing more focus on the expansive horizontalness of the structure. The geometric design of a three-window bay is now more central to the façade of the house. The steep, hipped roof with a wide overhang contains dormer windows, which themselves have hipped roofs with wide overhangs, a feature repeated by Wright throughout his lifetime.

Above: The plan of the house is conventional in layout and the living areas are distinctly compartmentalized. The hipped roofs have the familiar wide overhangs that Wright employed throughout many of his designs.

Right: Wright's last bootlegged house, the Goan House, appears to be clad in board-and-batten siding, but it is actually horizontal-patterned shingles.

FREDERICK BAGLEY HOUSE

Address: 121 South County Line Road, Hinsdale, Illinois
Built: 1894

This house is old by Hinsdale standards, a posh Chicago suburb that is currently undergoing an epidemic of teardowns, followed by the construction of massive mansions that is changing irrevocably the character of this tony enclave. The gambrel roof, or double sloping roof, is a central design feature of this handsome white Dutch Colonial revival house that sometimes is referred to as "Richardsonian Suburban." This is a style that owes its origins to the influence of Henry Hobson Richardson, the famed Boston architect whose work energized a whole generation of American architects hungry for a modern nineteenth-century American style. For the general layout of this house, Wright returned to the plan he used in his own Oak Park home—living-room reception area to the right of the entry, library beyond, with the dining room located at the far end of the house and a passage to the kitchen at the rear. Mr. Bagley, for whom this house was built, was a marble importer, which explains the uncharacteristic use of marble and stone here. In the interior, along a living-room wall, there is a marble-faced fireplace replete with an inglenook with marble Ionic columns.

The exterior of the house uses stone on the veranda and marble around the basement windows. Four Ionic columns of wood support the large overhang stretching over the veranda, a feature that indicates its important use in summer months, showing its centrality to the house. French doors lead to the interior off this spacious

Right: Frederick Bagley was a marble importer and indulged in a wide use of handsome marble and stone, unusual in a Wright dwelling.

porch that runs across the full face of the house. Set back on the north end of the structure is a robust, low-hipped, octagonal tower that serves as a library. Three large dormer windows across the face of the second floor are each gable-roofed. An elliptical eyebrow window (a familiar device used by Richardson) peeks from the right end of the third-floor dormer that originally was used as a servant's quarters. The horizontal cladding was originally shingled. Today, the horizontal sight lines created by that siding enhances the proportions of the house. The extended dormer roof adds powerful verticality to the view of the front of the house, while the open porch interjects a deepening of the horizontal profile. There is still a tactile feeling of the country in this house, more so than in many of Wright's dwellings. With both an attic and a basement, this house, however, would never qualify as one of Wright's "new houses," for they are precisely the first things to be jettisoned in his new conceptualization of the modern house.

Basements would remain "unwholesome" for him and attics "a useless height." Shadows of the Warren McArthur House on Kenwood Avenue in Chicago, built two years earlier, are easily recognizable here. Roof and dormer details are very similar. Though Wright employed double octagonal bays at each corner on the McArthur House, here that geometrical style is repeated for use in Bagley's library. Later, Wright would be influenced by this style yet again, drawing on it for the Mitchell residence in Racine, Wisconsin. They are contemporaneous structures whose commissions Wright announced together.

Above: Wright uses the geometry of the octagon in several early homes, including his own. Here, it lends itself well to Bagley's library.

ROLOSON ROWHOUSES

Address: 3213-3219 S. Calumet Avenue,
Chicago, Illinois
Built: 1894

This complex marks Wright's first apartment design and his only rowhouse design. They were executed for Robert Roloson, a successful Chicago grain merchant and the son-in-law of Wright's great benefactor, Edward C. Waller. There is a haunting, Sullivanesque touch in Wright's exterior embellishments on the façade of this elegant row of sophisticated Chicago townhouses. They belong to a great moment of the past, the era of the 1893 World's Columbian Exhibition that saw Chicago come of age as the nation's modern center. Imbued with the ethos of that World's Fair, Chicagoans had a taste for domestic residences of classical refinement. Each of these town homes is set on a ordinary twenty-five-foot city lot. After Roloson purchased them, he asked Wright to oversee their renovation. What emerged were four stately urban residences, startlingly refined in their gilded elegance. At four full stories each, they boasted interiors of more than 3,000 square feet. The handsome granite-exterior cladding and peaked, pagoda-like rooflines added a deeply graceful sense of proportion to each home. There is a poetic romanticism to their exaggerated size. Their large front doors and entranceways appear dwarfed by the sheer verticality of each building's upward sweep to the tip of the roofline. To accomplish his modernization of these period houses, Wright employed some touches here that he first introduced in the Charnley-Persky House. His use of golden, narrow, Roman brick, for instance, together with geometrically square window designs used on the fourth level and filigreed artistry separating the second and third floors are all effectively employed here. Great A-shaped gables form the recurring geometric character of the four structures.

Right: Among the features that Wright employed in the remodeling of the Roloson Rowhouses are the organic swirls of botanicals that separate the third and fourth levels, highly reminiscent of Louis Sullivan's design and Wright's previous aesthetic devotion to his mentor.

Above: The late-day sun kisses the tips of the gables on the Roloson Rowhouses, a remodeling executed in elegant Roman brick by Wright.

Opposite top: When Wright worked in the firm of Adler and Sullivan, it was said that his drawings were indistinguishable from Sullivan's, a point made more clear here by viewing his ornamentation of the Roloson Rowhouses heavy with graceful botanicals.

Opposite bottom: The heavy wooden door, limestone surround, and wheat-colored, narrow Roman brick on the façade of the Roloson Rowhouses.

1895

FRANCISCO TERRACE APARTMENTS

Address: Lake Street at Euclid Avenue, Oak Park, Illinois
Date: 1895

What you see here is not really the apartment complex designed by Wright in Chicago on the city's West Side. That structure was located in a neighborhood that has undergone substantial demographic change and urban deterioration. The original Francisco Terrace Apartments were commissioned by the wealthy Chicago real-estate speculator Edward Carson Waller and were located at 253 North Francisco Street between Walnut and Fulton streets, practically on top of Wright's Waller Apartment complex.

In 1895, there was a need for modern, multiple-unit urban dwellings that attempted to enhance life for young families in high-density communities. Wright developed this type of dwelling with the construction of the Francisco Terrace Apartments. This construction reflected the late nineteenth-century social genius for finding fresh ways to resolve urban dilemmas and Wright was supported in his endeavors by his patron, Waller.

Waller, a resident of River Forest, lived on Auvergne Place in that refined, leafy suburb, and was a neighbor of another of Wright's friends and clients, William Winslow. Waller was an important sponsor of two of Wright's projects (this apartment block and the Waller Apartments), in addition to the remodeling Wright carried out in his home that is now no longer standing. The commercially innovative Waller was interested in constructing low-cost, multiresidential, urban housing at the end of the nineteenth century. Waller's target market for this two-story apartment building, built around a central interior courtyard, was young married couples. So many newlyweds took advantage of this fresh idea in urban living that the complex became known as the "honeymoon terrace."

The entryway to the 175-foot-long courtyard was distinguished by an elegant terra-cotta arch executed in the familiar style of Wright's mentor and former employer Louis Sullivan. Entries to individual apartments were off the interior courtyard, giving residents an extra level of privacy and security, though front apartments could be entered from the street side. A wooden second-story balcony framed the interior garden courtyard and stairways were located within four towers at the interior corners. Most apartments had two bedrooms, a bathroom, a living room, and a kitchen, with entryways to the living rooms and kitchens throughout the complex.

Wright created a stunning rounded
entry arch for his Francisco Terrace
Apartments in Chicago in 1895.
Today this mighty example of
smooth proportion and symmetry
has been preserved, reset in a
contemporary apartment building
in Oak Park.

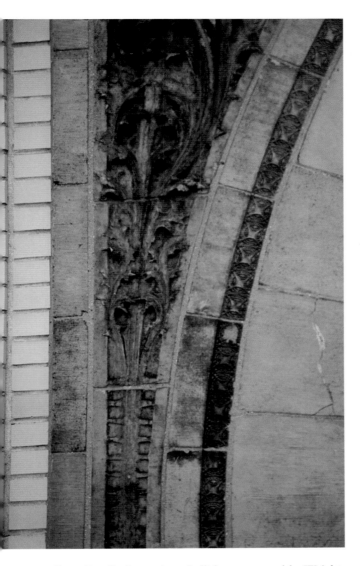

Above: Botanical ornamentation found on the entrance arch of the Francisco Terrace Apartments.

Above: Wright's original egg and dart molding from the Francisco Terrace Apartments is reminiscent of his copper ornamentation at the Charnley-Persky House.

Above: Detail of organic embellishment created by Wright for the Francisco Terrace Apartments arch, reminiscent of the hand of Louis Sullivan.

Left: Simple architectural treasures by Wright, rescued from the original Francisco Terrace Apartments, like this decorative stonework, transform the simplicity of its new home in Oak Park.

The apartments were eventually demolished in 1974, almost eighty years after they were first built. Wright's strategic sense of spatial utility and urban survival injected them with the resilience to stand against many eras of heavy use. Ultimately, they were destroyed, but not before the central archway that so distinguished their design could be rescued and reconstructed in Oak Park in 1977 in a new apartment complex. There, the infused sanctity of a Wright architectural artifact became the anchor of a whole new suburban residential project.

NATHAN G. MOORE HOUSE

Address: 333 Forest Avenue, Oak Park, Illinois
Built: 1895

Wright notes in his autobiography that after the Winslow House caused so much controversy due to its avant-garde design, "Mr. Moore did not want a house so 'different' that he would have to go down the back way to his morning train to avoid being laughed at." Moore went to Wright and wanted an expensive house designed in the Tudor style, at a time when Wright's family's financial needs were acute. Wright mentions his family responsibilities, some believe, as a way of deflecting criticism in designing such a revivalist-styled house. However, it is also known that Moore and Wright were kindred souls, sharing a love for music that often found Moore playing Wright's studio piano. Moore was a very successful Chicago attorney who, like other Wright clients, had membership in the Oak

Park Country Club. But in addition to playing golf, Moore was a fine photographer who added a darkroom to his list of necessities for inclusion within his new home. The house rose with high gables and half-timbered, casement windows with leaded diamond panes, re-creating, as it were, a piece of historic England along Forest Avenue, a street now thick with Wright inventions. After a fire in 1922 damaged the house, Moore asked Wright to build the house for a second time. Wright used what was left of the exterior walls, but he fashioned roofs that were far higher than the original's, giving the new house a look that was imbued more with his Asian-influenced artistry.

Left: Wright embellished the structure of this house with a style that is more reflective of his 1920s artistry, used in the postfire rebuilding of the structure, than his original late-nineteenth-century style Gothic revivalism.

Above: The multiple gables, Tudor stucco and wood banding, and ground-level ecclesiastical windows imbue the Moore House with a Gothic revivalism to which Wright applied his own special aesthetics.

CHAUNCEY L. WILLIAMS HOUSE

Address: 530 Edgewood
Place, River Forest, Illinois
Built: 1895

Wright brings out all his favorite architectural elements in this substantive domestic residence for Chauncey Williams along a historic leafy street. Great rows of trees line the lane, which is thick with other Wright houses (the Isabel Roberts House, among them) and other architecturally significant homes. Wright's steep, rough-shingled roof design gives a whimsical sense of country

Main picture: Wright demonstrated a bold Prairie aesthetic at the Chauncey Williams House early in his career, displaying in the design of this house many features that he repeated in later Prairie designs.

Left: The dormers are shielded by extensive projecting cantilevered roofs.

Right and far right: In contrast to the vertical pitch of the Williams House roof and dormers, Wright introduced an architecturally rich entry arch that demonstrates a unique symmetry and proportion. The large boulders that stretch along the lower portion of the house were brought from the banks of the nearby Des Plaines River.

This page: The soaring Roman brick chimney of the Williams House portrays an architectural symmetry that is balanced with the angular proportion of the bold roof pitch.

charm and an immediate sense of powerful verticality and geometric charm to this residence. The dramatic massing of the large Roman brick chimney is both aesthetic and utilitarian masonry, with the interior hearth a central axis of family life. It is an aspect of the domestic dwelling that would remain consistent throughout all Wright designs, from Prairie through Usonian. The horizontal plane of the house is reinforced by the use of thin, golden, wheat-colored Roman brick that rises from the base of the house to the sill line. Plaster clads the exterior walls from the brick to beneath the low-eave roofline. In 1900, five years after the house was built, Wright made alterations to the dormer, installing ventilation openings. His exterior alterations to the roof, then, gave greater emphasis to the horizontal quality of the structure. However, the present patterning of the roof's cedar shingles in a more uniform layering softens that and retains more of the original design.

The entryway surround is a significant piece of arching filigreed ironwork, reminiscent of the organic designs of Louis Sullivan, and used so effectively at the Charnley-Persky House. It is deeply evocative of the Prairie motif and a part of Wright's early aesthetic training. Williams was a man of charm and learning, a member of the Caxton Club of Chicago that counted other Wright clients, such as George Millard, among their antiquarian book collectors. The Edward C. Waller estate was just minutes away from the Williams House. It is from there that the large boulders used in the foundation work of the house are said to have come, removed from the banks of the Des Plaines River. It is said that Wright and Williams rolled the stones up from the river themselves.

EDWARD C. WALLER APARTMENTS

Address: 2840–2858 West Walnut Street, Chicago, Illinois

Built: 1895

Unlike the Francisco Terrace Apartments, located just behind these units, this Wright experiment in low-cost, multiresidential, urban housing has stood the test of time and continues to stand as an important link to the timeless designs of the past. Although this building was designed after the Francisco Terrace structure, it was built first and named for the man who brought them to life, Chicago real-estate mogul Edward C. Waller. Wright knew Waller not only professionally, but also socially. The great Chicago architect Daniel Burnham was a friend of Waller's and socialized at the Waller home in River Forest with the young Wright. In the Waller Apartments, there was genius at work. Originally, Wright designed five two-story buildings with each unit containing four separate apartments. Each apartment was modern in its compact utility and in the urban practicality of its design. Within each apartment, every tenant had a living room, dining room, bedroom, bathroom, and closet space. This interior space was very similar to the

Right: A side view of the Edward C. Waller Apartments is rich in modern symmetry that remains a powerful statement of architectural purpose. Large windows were an important feature of Wright's early treatment of urban multiple-family dwellings.

Left: The Edward C. Waller Apartments display a very modern massing of well-shaped brickwork, featuring a handsome entry arch of significant proportions.

design seen in the Francisco Terrace Apartments. For such moderate rental units, this was housing vastly superior to anything that was available in any other large American city.

It represented a significant refocusing of the whole notion of city living. Chicago had just welcomed twenty-six million people to the 1893 World's Columbian Exposition in which the modern character of Chicago was on view for all to see. The future had arrived already for most Chicagoans. So Wright and Waller were riding the crest of a spectacular rediscovery of what cities really could be for people. They were not just the hellholes of overcrowded tenements, they were also neighborhoods of civility and gracious beauty, as demonstrated in this forward-thinking apartment complex just a ten-minute trolley ride from downtown Chicago. The structures themselves carried Wright's familiar passion for elegance in brickwork with exterior embellishments found in the brickwork itself. The exterior framing of the flat, rectangular roofline is accomplished in a decorative banding of terra-cotta beading that further expands the geometric character into a fresh, contemporary, Prairie design of the exterior cladding. Entryways are set within a familiar Wright brickwork archway, a link to his mentorship with Louis Sullivan. A recess line of brickwork above the second-floor windows creates a horizontal brow line across the façade. Concrete banding beneath the first-floor sills heighten and expand the horizontal lines of the façade as well. A fire in 1968 gutted one of the units that later was demolished. Among the remaining four buildings, efforts continue to restore and revive the legacy of Wright that has survived for over a hundred years. The neighborhood now sits on the edge of fresh renewal as redevelopment fans out through the environs of the city's West Side. The city of Chicago keeps a special eye on this Wright treasure.

HARRISON R. YOUNG HOUSE: ADDITIONS AND REMODELING

Address: 334 N. Kenilworth Avenue, Oak Park, Illinois
Built: 1895

When Wright got his hands on this house, it had already been standing for some twenty years. First built in the 1870s by William E. Coman, Wright set out to transform it. His remodeling is significant for in it we are able to recognize some of the future elements that he would make so much a part of his modern Prairie design. Some significant structural work took place first

Far Left: Wright provided the Young House with extensive remodeling that brought the rich aesthetics of his Prairie design, most clearly demonstrated in the thin, narrow-band clapboard cladding.

Above: Small features like the second-story roof balcony provide the Young House with a strong sense of utility and grace. The soaring shingled roof design is emblematic of Wright's early work with Joseph Silsbee.

Left: Shapes of many interesting compositions intensify the architectural quality of the Young House, as well as its remarkably genteel and clean modernity during the age of Victorian clutter.

with the house being pushed back some sixteen feet more deeply into the lot. An addition was placed upon the façade of horizontal, narrow-band clapboard, familiar even at this early stage in Wright's work. A new living room, second-story bedrooms, and an expansive porch were a part of this new addition. So too was the sweeping overhang of the roof above the porch that Wright cantilevered over the entry drive. This would have had a utilitarian purpose when designed to permit access to a carriage during rain showers. The sweep of the eave gives the whole house a uniquely Wrightian character and a sense of modernity. The steeply pitched upper roof massing is reminiscent of the Clark House in LaGrange where the main A-frame peak is bisected by a perpendicular peak. Also like the Clark House, a narrow or Roman brick chimney rises tall and sleek above the rooftops. Such chimneys became almost emblematic of Wright's architecture throughout his career, expressive of the significance of the hearth in the detail of family life.

Above: Wright applied a gracious curving roof around the veranda of the Young House, intensifying its importance as a source of practical utility and high aesthetics. The buttressing of the extending roof permits it to provide both shelter and cover from the elements.

Left: The Young House once faced demolition but it was saved by a property company who later transferred the ownership to the University of Chicago. It is today a National Historic Landmark and one of the seventeen structures designed by Wright to have earned special recognition from the American Institute of Architects.

1896

CHARLES E. ROBERTS HOUSE: REMODELING

Address: 321 N. Euclid Avenue, Oak Park, Illinois
Built: 1896

This handsome Oak Park Queen Anne residence carries a doubly splendid Chicago architectural pedigree. First, the house was designed in 1879 by architect Daniel Burnham, whose hand guided so much revolutionary Chicago architecture such as the Reliance Building, the Monadnock Building, and ultimately the very "Plan for Chicago," the 1909 synthesis that set in motion Chicago's architectural future. The Roberts House was built in 1883. Then, thirteen years later, in 1896, Roberts asked Wright, a friend and Oak Park neighbor, to remodel the structure, imbuing it with a further historic provenance.

Roberts was a very successful businessman, the founder and president of the American Screw Company, the largest of its kind. But more importantly he was a man of creative invention, literally. He was responsible for the design of some of the most creative machines and products used in the business nationwide, as well as being the inventor of the Roberts electric car. His admiration for Wright's work came out of his own highly technical creative artistry. It was a friendship that endured and survived the worst of Wright's indiscretions. Wright

Right: The Charles E. Roberts House is as inventive as he was. Originally designed by noted Chicago architect Daniel Burnham, Wright remodeled the hefty Queen Anne structure for Roberts.

so admired Roberts that he named one of the rooms at Taliesin West in his honor. Roberts was also a member of the board at Unity Temple, and chiefly responsible for commissioning Wright to design his famed Prairie-style worship center for the Oak Park Unitarian community. Roberts remained a patron of Wright's, both artistic and financial, for many years. Wright in return went so far as to hire Roberts's daughter, Isabel, as his financial assistant, as well as designing a River Forest house for her.

In remodeling the Roberts House, Wright set out to quiet many of Burnham's exterior revivalist inclinations by reworking some of the details of the roof design, as well as the spacious wraparound front porch that has both significant utility and aesthetic effect. Wright gave the façade a crisp, modern look that is enhanced by the height of the horizontal cladding that rises up to the roofline. Diminutive, third-story, narrow, rectangular windows helped to refocus the proportions of the house, while Wright's unusually tall, narrow brick chimney also rearranged the scale of the roof massing. On the interior, the architect introduced a new first-floor bedroom at the front of the house and also redesigned the stairway on the first and second floors. For the central hearth in the family living room, Wright designed an American oak screen cabinet. This first commission for Charles Roberts represented the beginning of an important relationship of patronage for Wright. Some of his best work was done for Roberts and the many clients he brought to Wright. Some, like members of his wife, Mary's, family had Prairie houses of the highest quality designed for them. This was a lasting and profitable relationship for Wright and Roberts.

Left: Charles E. Roberts and his family were among the earliest residents of Oak Park. The introductions that Wright received through him in the 1890s were crucially important to the young architect.

HARRY C. GOODRICH HOUSE

Address: 534 N. East Avenue, Oak Park, Illinois
Built: 1896

Goodrich, like Charles Roberts, was an inventor, a genius at designing the apparatus and attachments used in sewing machines. In Wright, Goodrich too found an appealing sense of mechanical perfection. This commission offered Wright the opportunity to further expand his work away from the revivalist styles he so disliked. The design is actually a reworking of an idea Wright pitched to Charles Roberts for a series of low-cost homes. The project never came to fruition but Wright's adaptation of that original design was successful. The exterior skin of the house is horizontal board-and-batten, a form almost evocative of Wright's early designs. This narrow gauge cladding runs from the edge of the second-story windows down past the base of the structure; the result disguises the basement

that has been built just above the grade line. The proportion of the house is kept balanced by elements such as the second-story windows, which reach all the way up to the eave line. The three-section bay windows on both the first and second floors center the focus of the façade and compensate for the imbalance created by the porch at the north section of the façade. The roofline of the house and porch, each with wide overhangs, are complementary to each other and draw the powerful, double-pitched, upper roof into harmony with the whole structure.

Previous page: The profile of the Harry C. Goodrich House is intensified by Wright's soaring roof pitch and deeply projecting eaves. The proportion and symmetry of the façade is unified by the roof projections of the smaller porch roof.

Left: The roofline and gentle sloping of the Goodrich House's screened porch establishes balance and symmetry as essential elements of Wright's dramatic Prairie design.

GEORGE W. SMITH HOUSE

Address: 404 Home Avenue, Oak Park, Illinois

Built: 1896

Like the Goodrich House, this house, built for Marshall Field and Company employee George Smith, was originally designed as part of a series of low–cost homes for Charles Roberts to build in what was once known as Ridgeland and today is simply the eastern portion of Oak Park. This too is a variation of the Queen Anne style, but with unique Wrightian features that attempt to reshape the contours of that revivalist style. Lines,

singularly Wrightian, sweep across the steep, double-pitch roof with flared overhanging eaves. Two tall, slender, narrow, Roman brick chimneys stretch skyward and inject a familiar touch of the architect. The house has a decidedly horizontal sight line from the exterior cladding that looks as if it were board-and-batten, but in reality is a single row of shingles laid in a horizontal pattern. The aesthetic of the roof verticality and the horizontal exterior skin has a decidedly primitive first-generation New England quality to it, not unlike those mid-seventeenth-century board-and-batten structures in places like Dedham, Saugett, and Salem, in Massachusetts. The multiple peaks created from upper and lower roofs, as well as the dormers, create a lasting sense of focus that must have been startling in the last years of the nineteenth century. Oversized windows on the first floor help to reestablish an exciting sense of scale.

Left: The dramatically high-pitched roofs of the George Smith House, the graceful proportions of its flared overhangs, and the sturdy horizontal shingle cladding define its architectural character, while its soaring chimneys add a harmonious symmetry.

Below: An aerial perspective of the Smith House gives a significant view of its bulk and mass, as well as the graceful soar of its roofline.

ISIDORE HELLER HOUSE

Address: 5132 S. Woodlawn Avenue, Chicago, Illinois

Built: 1896

This house is a watershed structure for Wright. With this residence, designed for Chicago meatpacker Isidore Heller, he left behind the revivalist styles of the day for a design that was highly geometric and strikingly modern. No counterpart to this house could be seen on any other Chicago street at the time. Within its luxurious angularity and detail the architect's ever-deepening movement toward his ultimate Prairie consciousness could be seen. This is Wright's most outrageous design to date, but one that was perfectly understandable to those who witnessed the progressive evolution within his work throughout the decade. He gathered together all the elements of his new Prairie aesthetic here in the Heller residence, located in the Hyde Park neighborhood, just to the south of the Kenwood community on the city's South Side. Only recently incorporated into the City of Chicago, it sat within the footprint of the then-new University of Chicago with its elaborate American gothic designs by the young Henry Ives Cobb. Not far away along the lakeshore is Jackson Park, the site of the famed 1893 World's Columbian Exposition that included Sullivan's triumphant arched Transportation Building, executed by Wright's own hand.

The Heller House is Wright's first Hyde Park design. It was later followed by his Prairie apotheosis, the Robie House, just six blocks away. Wright's architectural voice soars in the sweeping drama of the Heller House. A powerful geometric flourish weaves through his design, displaying a natural absorption of the ethos of Louis Sullivan. There is great artistic exploration at work in this commission. The house is fashioned out of yellow Roman brick that gives a delicate horizontal character to the exterior, though it carries the eye ever upward by a graceful and stunningly flat angularity. The wide chimney of Roman brick was by now a regular feature of his work, but still retains both its utility and beauty by its practical verticality. Since the building sits sideways to conform to the narrow size of its city lot, the entrance is located on the side of the house. Wright embellished the entry with an abundance of rich, textured classical ornament. Above the entry lintel, deeply cantilevered, a stone panel holds three decorative quatrefoils with organic decorative designs. The lintel massing sits atop two stone columns with ornately rich, organic capitals, Wright's

Above: An aerial view of the Heller House shows its enormously long, narrow form sitting sideways from the street with elegantly proportioned rooflines, extended eaves, and massive chimney blocks.

Right: One of Wright's most elegant and substantive early Chicago Prairie homes is fashioned of architecturally sophisticated, narrow, golden, Roman brick.

Prairie addition to the five orders cataloged by Palladio. Wider stone framing, projecting around the entryway, squares off the space.

The girth of the house faces the street and projects a sense of verticality by the many staggered levels of design—the roof plateaus, as well as the projections formed by the brick and stonework. Broad roofs with deep overhangs are above the second and third floors. The scaling back of the third floor gives both proportion and modern elegance to the house. An elaborate classical plaster frieze frames the roofline along the third floor. It was designed and executed by the artist Richard Bock and established a curious European lyricism around the house. Maidens, with naked forms thinly veiled, dance together, linked hand-to-hand, around the highly romantic, open loggia high atop the third-floor level. Windows on the street side sit within a stoneclad wall. The use of such material adds to the vertical rise. Horizontal perspective is added by the addition of a white-stone string coursing, or narrow banding, that encircles the house just below the second-story sills. The geometry of the house is enhanced by the deliberate placement of the windows that strengthens the exterior harmony. In a neighborhood so forested with university faculty and erudite classical scholars, this mini palazzo was an ideal fit. It might not have worked, however, in many other Chicago neighborhoods in 1896.

Left: The third story of the Heller House is encrusted with sculptured figures by the noted designer Richard Bock, creating a miniature palazzo not far from the University of Chicago.

Above: The second story of the Isidore Heller House is rich in organic ornamentation and brick pillars that add nobility and elegance to the structure.

CHARLES E. ROBERTS STABLE

Address: 317 N. Euclid Avenue, Oak Park, Illinois
Built: 1896

This handsome house has a curious English feel to it, like one of the great country homes designed by renowned architect Sir Edward Luytens. The massing of the great roof and the staggering proportions of the double-brick chimneys demonstrate a luxe style that ushered modernity into the posh, aristocratic English countryside when Luytens, the darling of the smart set, was reshaping country life. Wright and Luytens shared a part of the world stage of architecture for a time and each had a penchant for remarkable brickwork design. Wright transformed this structure from a barn into a modern structure for the inventive Charles Roberts, fashioning a suitable home for Roberts's electric car. Roberts's capacity for modern inventions was at the heart of his commercial success as a manufacturer. As one of Wright's most established patrons, Roberts shared Wright's passion for the emerging modern world that was quickly breaking into their comfortable Oak Park world. Electricity was altering the ordinary lives of people and Roberts was quick to adapt his resourcefulness to the possibilities that electric energy could provide.

Roberts's horseless carriage was one such phenomenon of engineering. Its impact was sufficient to entitle his invention to its own special laboratory, a former barn reinvented by Wright's creativity. So significant was Wright's design that sometime later, between 1903 and 1905, Roberts's son-in-law, the architect Charles E. White, who worked in the Wright studio and was married to Alice Roberts, converted the stable into a residence. The former stable was

Left: Wright remodeled the stable at the Charles Roberts House and transformed it into a picturesque structure imbued with a cozy, country expression and a decidedly expressive sense of modernity with its soaring, high-pitched gabled roof and towering chimney.

Right: Detail of Wright's reworking of the stable.

physically moved in 1929 to its present nearby location from the rear of the Roberts House, at which time it received the designation of its present address.

The remarkable upward sweep of the house's verticality expresses a dominant sense of shelter and safety that is often conveyed in the large protective overhangs of Wright's roof designs. The sheer scale of the roof, with dormer windows at the second-story level, is balanced by the solid vertical lift of the two chimneys that sit on each side of the house. Wright's architectural thumbprint is still visible despite the successive design themes introduced by White. This is a handsome structure and a residence that instantly expresses a familial coziness that often is included in Wright's more inventive architectural designs. Wright's sweeping alterations took this structure from barn to opulent shelter for the namesake invention of Charles Roberts. In the waning days of the nineteenth century, this was a fortuitous leap and an extraordinary exercise in design on Wright's part and artistic patronage on Roberts's part. Charles White, having absorbed the ethos of his mentor within the studio, carried his design one step further into this Cotswaldian residence.

Above: The Charles Roberts Stable has had a long history of redesign from Wright's early transformation of an old barn into a garage/laboratory for the inventive Roberts to its later reconfiguring into a domestic residence by Roberts's architect son-in-law.

Wright introduced an aesthetic
of remarkable angularity in his
remodeling of the Roberts Stable
that transformed it into a structure
of delicate country charm and
modernity.

1897

 GEORGE FURBECK HOUSE

Address: 223 N. Euclid Avenue, Oak Park, Illinois
Built: 1897

The career of Frank Lloyd Wright entered a curious period of architectural experimentation in the commissions he received from Warren Furbeck, a wealthy Oak Park stockbroker who was a close friend of Wright's patron Charles Roberts. The Furbecks further expanded the remarkable network of Wright's clients that were a web of financially successful, artistically sophisticated individuals with the capacity to appreciate and anticipate the modernity of Wright's artistry. They certainly stood outside the mainstream of their contemporaries. They appeared to express a similar personal aestheticism more in harmony with that of Chicago's undisputed society ruler, Bertha Palmer, whose vast collection of French Impressionists was another demonstration of edgy, Prairie, avant-garde taste. In Chicago, vast fortunes often begat refined taste. In the last three years of the nineteenth century, Wright reached an important synthesis in his architectural design. This last breath of the century represented a time of critical personal experimentation for him that brought an end to his early period of architectural speculation and Prairie design incubation.

The Furbeck designs culminated in two substantial residences that were wedding gifts from Warren Furbeck to his sons, who both married in 1897. The first of these, a large, light, rose-hued brick residence, was designed for George W. Furbeck, the oldest of the Furbeck sons. It uses some design elements that are familiar from Wright's portfolio. For instance, two substantial octagonal towers frame the exterior façade of the house and influence the interior footprint of the house. Wright's Emmond House in LaGrange, with its own double-octagonal towers, and his Thomas Gale and Robert Parker houses on Chicago Avenue in Oak Park, each with one octagonal tower bay, prefigured his more elaborate use of the eight-sided towers here. None of these towers, however, were fashioned of the more visually cumbersome brick. Flanking the entry as they do, the towers dominate the façade, while the use of common brick overexaggerates their massing and gives the structure a beefy, portly rotundity. The multiple hipped-roof surfaces appear to sit saucerlike, rising above the horizontally elongated hipped-roof design used above the entrance. In 1920, this open entranceway underwent rebuilding as an enclosed brick porch, further bulking up the exterior lines, with the result that it now looks like it received the addition of a small brick 1950s bungalow as an afterthought. A considerably more expansive third-floor dormer redesign was also included at this time. Soaring, rectangular, double chimneys are repeated here, another of Wright's familiar and

increasingly more permanent architectural features. Within the interior, the main reception area is octagonal, shaped by the form of the tower and containing a substantial fireplace, which along with the second hearth between the dining room and the kitchen, was also quickly to become an established feature of Wright's style. The importance of the hearth carried both utilitarian and social features for Wright, who imbued them with an almost tribal significance for their ability to gather and energize the family. George Furbeck had little appreciation of this house and moved out in less than two years.

Above: The George Furbeck House was one of a pair of homes designed by Wright as wedding gifts to the sons of Warren Furbeck. This house has extensive massing and girth, almost uncharacteristic of Wright, most notably demonstrated in the powerful, close brickwork and twin front towers.

ROLLIN
FURBECK
HOUSE

Address: 515 N. Fair Oaks
Avenue, Oak Park, Illinois
Built: 1897

This was another of Warren Furbeck's wedding gifts for one of his sons, Rollin. In many ways, this is a house far superior to the one designed for brother George. Once again, Wright was engaged in a personal synthesis during this period of design experimentation up until the turn of the century. This house, of soft, golden, common brick, demonstrated Wright's willingness to repeat and expand on successful design motifs previously used. Here, the shadow of his hugely successful Heller House in Hyde Park fell across this project in Oak Park. The result, however, is a decidedly more expansive residence, sprawling across a spacious piece of elevated property. Its size gave the architect none of the complexities that his Heller House required because of its narrow city space.

Wright repeated in the Rollin Furbeck House the graceful verticality that rose with such dramatic proportionality at the Heller House. The refined addition of classical columns on the upper level of the residence is less complex than the more elaborate ones on Heller's open loggia. But Wright challenged the eye here in much the same way by his graceful setbacks floor by floor. While the house has a soaring vertical ascent, it is also a very horizontal structure. These sight lines are enhanced by the multiple levels of hipped roofs that span the first floor's cruciform arms, as well as the open front porch. The second-floor roof wings project on either side of the central tower. Finally, the third floor rises high, its center capped with a hipped roof scaled to its size. Wide

Above: The Rollin Furbeck House has considerably more vertical lift than the George Furbeck House. Proportion and symmetry add a particularly grand grace and elegance to this large, baronial residence with broad, hipped roofs.

overhangs at every level reinforce the angularity of this grand house. This house was an important link for Wright between the transitional stages of his own architectural development showing his maturation from square and rectangular plans in his early designs to his more expansive cruciform and pinwheel designs used so significantly in his later plans.

The exterior horizontal character of the house is also expanded by the use of large horizontal picture windows running across the first-floor façade in the living room and dining room. This was Wright's first use of such large architectural window treatments in a domestic residence. He continued to mold the geometry of the exterior by his controlled design of upper-floor windows whose shapes enhance the total façade, much like he did at the Charnley House. At the sill break between the first and second floors, Wright used generous Bedford limestone capping off the brick projection and ran a limestone course here, as well as between the second and third floors, furthering the horizontal symmetry of the design. The house has received gracious restoration of its most important design features and remains well cared for. This is one of Wright's most gracious homes, baronial and friendly, though not for Rollin Furbeck, who left this paternal wedding gift even faster than his brother George left his.

Above left: Detail of an upper area of the Rollin Furbeck House demonstrates the refined application of pillars and diamond-paned, leaded windows with which Wright fashioned this massive Prairie masterpiece with aesthetic parallels to the Heller House.

Above right: The front portico of the Rollin Furbeck House is an important part of the façade, holding its concealed entranceway.

Above: From a side view, the true proportions of the Rollin Furbeck House can be seen. Elegant, narrow, mustard-yellow, Roman brickwork has power and grandeur.

FRANK LLOYD WRIGHT'S LIFE 1890-1899

Wright's early Chicago years provided him with an extraordinary architectural education. Louis Sullivan, one of the city's most valued architects and just ten years Wright's senior, led him into extraordinary opportunities that reconfigured his architectural character. Sullivan appears to have seen himself in the young apprentice and appreciated Wright's innate artistry and fluidity of technique. Wright's drawings were often indistinguishable from Sullivan's, so in sync were their aesthetic sensibilities. Each was born with the rarest of gifts, the ability to conceive images in three dimensions.

Perhaps nothing in the period of Wright's employment with the firm of Adler and Sullivan had a more significant impact on the young draftsman than Sullivan's design for the Transportation Building of the World's Columbian Exposition of 1893. Famed Chicago architect Daniel Burnham had been chosen to head the overall design team for the international celebration held along the south lakefront in Jackson Park, near the present home of the University of Chicago. Burnham had prestige and the high status of a serious American architect. So he stunned many when his designs for the Exposition reflected a revivalist classical style. It was uncharacteristically un-American with its domes, columns, and peristyles—more a reflection of ancient Greece and Rome. Wright has the distinction of working on the only non-neoclassical building with Sullivan, the stunning Prairie simplicity of the Transportation Building. Wright inked all of Sullivan's designs reflecting the rich, organic movement of his signature style. Their work was the talk of the fair and a tactile expression of hope that American designs could hold their own with the revivalist styles.

This was also a period of tremendous personal change in Wright's life. While attending Sunday services at his uncle Jenkin Lloyd Jones's All Saints Unitarian Church, the young man met a young woman in the congregation, Catherine Tobin, with whom he fell in love. She was only seventeen at the time. Despite the protestations of family on both sides and close friends, the couple married. Adler and Sullivan, however, presented no such opposition. Instead, they offered Wright a five-year contract that gave him the resources to wed. So supportive was Sullivan that he personally loaned Wright the money to design and build a house in the cozy, western

Right: Louis Sullivan was a significant influence on the young Frank Lloyd Wright during his early years in Chicago.

Wright designed the Romeo and Juliet windmill in 1896. The plan reveals a diamond interlocked with an octagon. The original wood shingles were replaced with horizontal boards and battens in 1939.

suburb of Oak Park against his contract with the firm. Wright built a remarkable house of brick and shingles in the Arts and Crafts style, very much reflecting his American aesthetic ideal. This would be Wright's home for the next twenty years with his beautiful wife, Catherine, and their six children, four boys and two girls. Oak Park was to be the making of Wright and later, the breaking of him. He would find fame along its leafy streets and many clients among its quiet, inventive citizens.

During this period, Wright was displaying the personal colorful demeanor that would forever display his genius. Back at the office, as chief draftsman, some four dozen men worked under Wright, though there was never any doubt he was the apple of Sullivan's eye. He had his unquestioned trust and friendship. They were in tandem, sharing the excitement and anticipation of what the "modern" was unleashing on the world. More than anything else, they shared the common belief that architecture must evolve in total harmony with its use. The dramatic beauty of the Charnley-Persky House, etched with Prairie character, was an 1891 triumph of the Sullivan-Wright partnership.

However, during this period of personal happiness and professional success, Wright began to supplement his income by designing houses on the side. These homes, many still lived in today in suburban Oak Park, represent some of his earliest and most substantive achievements architecturally. In moonlighting while on the Adler and Sullivan payroll, he was breaking the cardinal rule of the firm. Often he signed plans under the name of his earliest Chicago friend, architect Cecil Corwin. Many of these early houses reflect the Queen Anne style that was so popular at the time. Sullivan, however, discovered his secret activity sometime in 1893 and fired Wright. It was a bitter break. Wright retreated to his studio in his Oak Park home and proceeded to shape an independent career.

The 1893 W. H. Winslow House in the western suburb of River Forest has the distinction of being Wright's first great independent commission and his first Prairie-style house. The design was a radical departure from conventional plans of the day. The young architect's career was buoyed by an additional fifteen unique designs in Chicago and the surrounding suburbs before the turn of the century. Each moved Wright closer to his aesthetic imperative of architecture influenced by and in harmony with its natural setting.

1900

WILLIAM
ADAMS HOUSE

Address: 9326 S. Pleasant
Avenue, Chicago, Illinois
Built: 1900

The sheer horizontal brick bulk of this house, with its extraordinary hipped-roof angularity, luxuriously deep overhangs, low-roofed horizontal front porch, dormer overhangs, and chimneys, presents a very tailored, modern, baronial Prairie prototype. In the wooded, leafy north end of Chicago's Beverly Hills neighborhood, it is a perfect fit.

William Adams was a successful contractor whose clients were some of Chicago's most prestigious architects, from Howard Van Doren Shaw to Richard E. Schmidt and Hugh Garden, as well as Adler and Sullivan. Adams began a professional collaboration with Wright sometime around 1895 and was engaged in the project of constructing the Winslow Stables in River Forest. Adams also worked on the Heller House in Hyde Park. But, it was perhaps the massive Husser House along the Chicago lakefront, demolished in 1926, that was their ultimate success. Adams and Wright had a remarkable relationship in that Wright often found it difficult to find contractors who were willing to work on his edgy designs or put up with his complicated details. The very name of Wright on a blueprint was enough to

Right: The Adams House sits deep in the leafy texture of Chicago's Beverly Hills neighborhood, a refined "country in the city" community.

114

THE
WILLIAM ADAMS
HOUSE
BUILT 1900
ARCHITECT
FRANK LLOYD WRIGHT
9326 PLEASANT AVE.
Ridge
HISTORIC DISTRICT

9326

Above: **Wright's designs for Prairie art glass were simple and geometric, accentuating the creation of a unique American style and the aesthetic pleasure of interior living as exterior.**

send many contractors running. Adams had no such reticence. It is curious that with all his contacts with some of the most well-known architects in Chicago, that Adams should have gone to Wright for the designs of a new house he wished to build. Wright's commission of the Adams residence is a testament to Adams's appreciation of Wright's work.

The house has particular significance today because of the sense of prefiguring that so many elements of the house display. Nothing shows that more than the expansive front porch that Wright reestablished as a connector between interior space and exterior space, rather than the usual Victorian utility of an outdoor room. Wright uses the porch to expand the unity of the structure to include its setting in nature. Most windows at the Adams House are of the double-hung variety, not particularly well liked by Wright. He was dissatisfied with the way the sash cut into the view. His solution here was to treat the two halves unevenly, narrowing the upper window and expanding the lower portion for an unobstructed view. Wright embellished the upper windows with elegant geometric caning and Prairie art glass. It is believed that the Adams-Wright relationship did not survive the strain resulting from the frequent clashes over design changes during the Adams House construction. The present owner's parents purchased the house in 1952 and attempted to correspond with Wright to learn more about the house's history. Sadly, he never responded to their inquiries, fueling speculation that he wanted to distance himself from this project even after half a century. He would be surprised today by the house's vibrancy and fresh character that remains dramatically elegant and reservedly genteel.

Above: Detail of Wright's delicate window design of simple geometric patterning highlighted by tiny diamonds of opaque color.

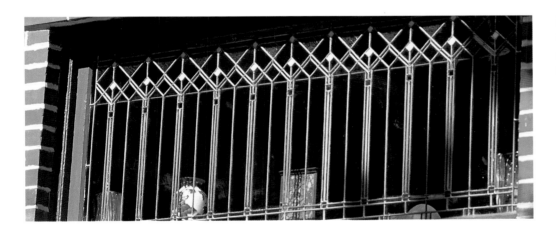

Left: Windows have high artistry in Wright's Prairie style—caming is usually in zinc with geometric Prairie motifs.

Left: An exterior lamp in the Prairie style with simple zinc banding created a geometric light fixture that was bold and fresh at the time Wright fashioned the Adams House.

S. A. FOSTER HOUSE AND STABLE

Address: 12147 S. Harvard Avenue, Chicago, Illinois
Built: 1900

This handsome residence is located in a Chicago neighborhood known as West Pullman, on the city's southern side. It is among Wright's most imaginative designs for a domestic residence. Originally built in 1900 for Chicago attorney and later circuit court judge Stephen Foster, the house was later sold to Sophie Ykema Roberts, whose family has had continued ownership of the house for the past ninety years. Built as the century turned, the house displays Wright's passionate taste for Japanese artistry, though his design was produced before his first trip to Japan. Wright, however, had already come under the influence of Japanese aesthetics through his avid collecting of Japanese prints. The lavish, sweeping rooflines that flare with so much delicacy in classical Japanese art prints are reflected in the steep-pitched elegance of the Foster House roofs.

Wright's design was for a country house, set in what was then verdant countryside some fifteen miles from downtown Chicago at the dawn of the twentieth century. This was the Prairie-scape of rural Cook County, and sitting with high elegance, there was Wright's masterpiece of Prairie design. Marcia Tharp, the great-granddaughter of Sophie Ykema Roberts notes that her family had a local dairy business in those days.

Whenever they would pass the Foster House, they would comment on its extraordinary beauty and design. They fell in love with it. So committed were they to live there that they sold their milk business and their entire dairy herd, pooled their financial resources with other relatives, and, finally, purchased the house. Four generations resided there. Tharp recalls the family lore in which Wright paid a visit to the house and

Above: The simplicity of Wright's pagoda roofs on the Foster House in Chicago has made it a neighborhood curiosity for a century. Set on six city property lots, it is an expansive urban estate.

Left: The upward angularity of the Foster House roof is an element of architectural genius in this masterpiece of urban design.

became furious with her great-grandmother because she had placed draperies on the windows.

Japanese touches begin at the very entrance to the house in the soaring lines of the pillar caps that top the posts forming the entryway. Younger family members recall that other children referred to the house as the "Chinese gambling house." The house emerged at the dawn of Wright's transition from early experimentation to his Prairie years. He was never more delightfully experimental than with the Foster House. The house faces north, turned from the street, with the main entrance off the side driveway sheltered by a large extending eave, giving added privacy. The result is exposures that let an ample amount of sunlight through the many windows along the east and west sides of the house. The rambling porch at the rear was the center of family life in the summer. During the winter, the arched fireplace became the main focus of family life. It was a house filled with expansive light that remains fondly in the memories of those who grew up there. The sweeping verticality of the roof peaks is balanced by the horizontal line created by the shingled cladding and horizontal board.

Above: **The entrance to the Foster House compound is through a pagoda-themed gateway that reinforces the unique Asian aesthetics of the structure.**

Above: Wright's delicate Asian nuance is used to great effectiveness in the roofline and angular pitch of the Foster House.

Right: Multiple roofs jut out from the sleek, dramatic, soaring angularity of the Foster House, providing a unique sense of shelter and protection.

1901

FRANK THOMAS HOUSE

Address: 210 Forest Avenue, Oak Park, Illinois

Built: 1901

This large L-shaped Oak Park house has two peculiar significances to it. First, it represented another house designed by Wright as a wedding gift for the offspring of a client. Secondly, the Thomas House represented a new age in domestic architecture, as well as a new era for Wright's designs, as it was his first fully mature Prairie house. James C. Rogers, a friend of Wright's, built the house as a present for his daughter and son-in-law, Mr. and Mrs. Frank Thomas. Frank Thomas, also a friend of Wright's, was a successful stockbroker and member of the Chicago Board of Trade. He was also an avid golfer, a founding member of the Oak Park Country Club, and, like Wright, a member of the River Forest Tennis Club, for whom the architect would later design a building.

Wright introduced many design features here that were to become, eventually, standard elements in his domestic architecture. For Wright, the age of experimentation had come to an end and he embarked on a solid expression of singular American artistry.

Right: The art-glass bejeweled interior entrance to the Thomas House shimmers with a remarkable artistry shaped by Wright's ability to capture natural light and use it effectively.

Above: The Thomas House appeared
so exotic and architecturally
mysterious that Oak Parkers called
it "the Harem." Wright ushered
in a new age of architecture in this
American masterpiece of unusual
horizontal profile.

In the Thomas House, Wright discovered a voice within him that strongly influenced all his future work. For instance, Wright built without either a basement or an attic, two features for which he had little use. Instead, he compensated by lifting the basement above ground, incorporating ample accommodations for house staff, and then raising the living areas of the house up to the second level, ensuring an extra layer of practicality and privacy needed for such a big house on such a small lot. In addition, this lifting addressed a very utilitarian necessity, providing optimum access to the very best in unobstructed natural ventilation. Another breakthrough feature is that the exterior walls of the house were fashioned entirely of stucco, or composite plaster, and were a first for Wright in Oak Park. This element became an important feature of his Prairie style. Plaster provided him with a design flexibility not found in exterior wood cladding. With stucco, he was able to achieve just the right geometric contouring on a house of frame design. Wright introduced an entryway off the street that began with passage through an expansive arch and wound through a mazelike corridor ending up on the second level's veranda. So exotic did this

arch appear on the façade of the Thomas House that Oak Park residents took to calling it "the Harem." The L-shaped design consisted of a long two-story wing horizontal to the street and a one-story section that was perpendicular to it. The large massing of the lower stucco walls rearranged the proportion of the house and the narrow, loggialike veranda introduced a graceful scale by its low, hipped roof with deep eaves extending along the second-floor level. It dramatically expanded the horizontal character of the house, as did the reduced upper level with horizontal string coursing and similar deep eave overhangs. The upper level contains the family bedrooms and is reflective of a similar design Wright liked to use in later Usonian designs in which he separated public and private areas within a house. There is a very crisp Asian sensibility within the house that grew more predominant in Wright's later work. Remarkable art glass complements the design, sparkling in gold. Wright also included some custom furniture for the Thomas House, which became more and more a feature of his Prairie residences. This house marked an important moment in Wright's architectural fusion between function and aesthetics.

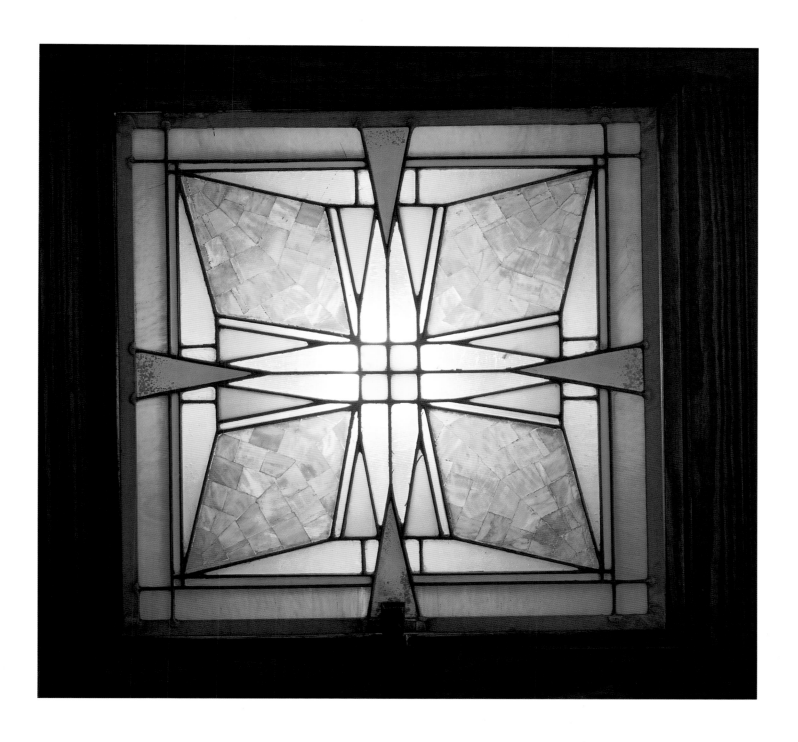

Opposite page: To reach this exotic entrance at the Thomas House, one first had to navigate the almost hidden entry passage, a maze of right-angled, hidden devices to extend privacy from the street.

Above: A detail of one of Wright's most luxurious art-glass windows. The colors used are the architect's warmest Prairie-style hues, evocative of the flatland geography.

WILLIAM G. FRICKE HOUSE

Address: 540 Fair Oaks Avenue, Oak Park, Illinois
Built: 1901

This is an important house, designed for William Fricke, the secretary of the C. F. Weber Company, who only resided here for some five years. It is another example of Wright's important early Prairie-style domestic residences. Like the Thomas House, it is an all-stucco house. Turned sideways along Iowa Street, it takes full advantage of the width of this corner lot. Certainly its outstanding distinction can be said to be its soaring height. This is a great, tall house that expressed an architectural maturity in Wright that was almost tactile, a design form that was emerging throughout the previous decade. This is a house of sweeping angularity, largely generated by the roof plateaus and horizontal banding spaced across the surface to enhance the horizontal character of the façade. At the same time, these horizontal sight lines help expand the lift of the structure's verticality. Wright was able to achieve this remarkable exterior massing by his use of stucco on the exterior skin. Once again, he was able to foster his desired perspective and proportion through his sculptured application of stucco, something he could not accomplish with wooden cladding. With stucco, he dramatically intensified the structure's verticality and its powerful linear projection. Low, hipped roofs with expansive overhangs and thin edges helped to generate the sense of towering mass and appeared to form flowing plateaus across the surfaces of each level of the house.

At the very top of what is the central core of the structure, square loggia windows were open, or unglazed, and framed the three-story tower created by the upward sweep of three long, vertical, narrow-paned windows that soared above the central entranceway. It was a familiar element, seen before at both the Heller House

Below: Wright's early Prairie masterpiece, the Fricke House in Oak Park, is among his most lofty dwellings for its height and soaring size. Its flat, expansive roofs add a dramatic modernity and architectural nobility that is fresh and inventive.

Above: The Fricke House, as seen from Fair Oaks Avenue, a side projection that gives an interesting view of the many levels of its rich, horizontal framing and geometric massing.

and the Rollin Furbeck House. Similar small, square loggia windows were also effectively employed, here, below the roofline, and above the string banding at the west end of the house along Fair Oaks Avenue. Their cubelike design was reminiscent of Wright's effective window design at the Charnley-Persky House, almost ten years earlier. A second front entrance, with tall double doors, was set behind a short wall at this west, or frontal, side of the house. Along the central Iowa Street façade, a pointed, triangular bay window and triangular stucco projection above it, which contained the living room and reception area, intensified this exterior angularity. The characteristic of the stucco and contrasting exterior banding would go on, with Wright, to receive adaptation and revision, ultimately becoming an essential construct of his Prairie style. Repeated versions of it helped solidify his superior reputation in creating distinctive homes in which geography, function, and aesthetics fused. As with the Thomas House, Wright continued his practice of placing built-in furniture throughout the house. Some design elements are recognizable in later adaptations for other Prairie-style homes. For instance, at the William Martin House in Oak Park, the dynamic horizontal planes found in the Fricke

House appear once again. And while the Martin House, too, soars with a similar grace encompassed in single-story, two-story, and three-story sections, the central tower developed for Fricke was not to be repeated elsewhere as a Prairie element. In the bold surface of the exterior walls, a shadow of the later design for Unity Temple can be seen in embryo. William Fricke only remained in residence here for some five years before he left, following a variety of matrimonial problems. The second owner, Emma Martin, purchased the home in 1906. A garage that reflects the style and proportions of the house was added in 1907. Wright equipped it with a second-story room, replete with a hearth.

Above: A multitude of expressive, projecting planes gives the Fricke House its unique celebrity on a corner lot that enables Wright's design to be seen in its fullest perspective.

Right: The house features one of Wright's most dramatic expressions of vertical lift from its ground-floor entrance along Iowa Street to its lofty loggia high atop the fourth story of the structure.

F. B. HENDERSON HOUSE

Address: 301 S. Kenilworth Avenue, Elmhurst, Illinois
Built: 1901

In the cozy, leafy community of Elmhurst, southwest of Oak Park, Wright yet again rendered another splendid, fresh, Prairie house in a year in which he appeared to have found an architectural voice of both magnitude and substance. The Henderson House is dynamic—evocative of the prairie landscape on which it sits. Wright commented on the geographical bonding of house and land in his Prairie design at the time: "The house began to associate with the ground and became natural to the prairie site." This house demonstrates that intimacy concretely. None of this is an accident. Instead, it was the conscious product of Wright's vision. At the Henderson House, Wright stated that he reduced the scale of the structure, a change recalibrating further renderings of this increasingly familiar stucco-surfaced design. While the Henderson House does not soar as steeply as the Fricke House, it expands outward with even more gracefully defined, sweeping, hipped roofs; broad eaves; and deep, gently sloping overhangs. For Wright this represented the achievement of

Wright recalibrates the scale of his Prairie design at the Henderson House without sacrificing any of its elegance of form and proportion. Its projecting roof plateaus give the dwelling a horizontal character and gave it modernity at the turn of the nineteenth century.

two essential goals for the Prairie house design—providing shelter against the elements and preservation of the stucco walls. Wright reinterpreted his Prairie house form here. For instance, he noted that the walls at the Henderson House began low, on the water table that served as a flat platform and then were lifted up to the second story, all the way to the line of the windowsill. He then sheathed the area above this with sets of windows that became a stunning feature of Prairie design. At this point he achieved another of his goals of Prairie design, the diffusion of reflected light throughout the upper level of the family bedrooms.

The house sits sideways on a very spacious corner lot, like the Fricke House, providing ample room for the sweeping horizontal massing of the house. Among the more remarkable design characteristics is the curious main entryway in which the proportions of the overheightened lower-porch columns dwarf human scale, rising to enfold everyone as they enter. Shelter on a grand scale occurs instantly as soon as one begins to walk up the entrance stairs to the main level, located a full story above ground and serving as the living level. Tucked away at ground level, to the side of the entryway, is another entrance into the service areas, used originally by staff. At both the east and west wings of the house pentagonal projections contain the living room and dining area;

Above: The vertical lift of the Henderson House is complemented by the horizontal lines created by the trim banding. Here, a private side-entry door is hidden from the street by the wall of Prairie spindles and stucco pillar.

the windows show richly textured Prairie art glass of quality. The Henderson House has a twin in the Warren Hickox House in Kankakee, Illinois (relatives of Charles Roberts's wife). On the Hickox House, however, Wright made an alteration by using a gabled roof, rather than a hipped roof. Wright's acknowledged collaboration of this house with architect Webster Tomlinson adds another curious patina to the house, as this was the only "partner" Wright ever claimed to have.

Above: The main entrance to the Henderson House provides significant privacy from the street by the high stucco walls that shield the stairs and front door, which is set deeply beneath the sheltering entry roof.

Left: The garden of the Henderson House holds a copy of one of Wright's "sprites" from his Midway Gardens, the Chicago beer garden of 1913.

WARD W. WILLITS HOUSE

Address: 1445 Sheridan Road, Highland Park, Illinois
Built: 1901

This is Frank Lloyd Wright's first North Shore house, as the countrified environs far north of Chicago are known. These suburbs are not only leafy, they also border on the lakeside and enjoy that ultimate treasured glimpse from off the prairie, the waters of Lake Michigan. Wright could have found no more gracious stretch of beauty on which to place an important house than this. The Ward Willits House is considered by many to be the very first Prairie-style house designed by Wright. And while other houses, like the Thomas House and even the Winslow House, vie in contention for that title, this is certainly the finest "masterpiece" of Wright's maturing, early Prairie designs. Its sheer size and opulence, together with the high refinements of Wright's design, guarantee that. Willits was the president of an important brass and bronze foundry, the Adams and Westlake Company. His company made artistic contributions to many projects of architectural significance.

Above: **Wright achieves a high architectural grandeur in his Prairie masterpiece, the Ward Willits House. His stucco walls soar and his rooflines project with symmetry and grace.**

The artist Orlando Giannini, whose work for Wright in both art-glass design and murals is still considered among the architect's very best, was employed by Willits. It is speculated that it was originally through Giannini that Wright met Willits. It was a fortuitous meeting in any event, for not only did Willits commission Wright to design a baronial Prairie-style house for him in Highland Park, but he went on to become a close friend and patron of Wright, even to the point of accompanying the architect on his first trip to Japan in 1905, as well as financing the journey. Communication between Wright and Willits was often strained during the construction phase of this project by Wright's lack of availability for consultation during critical moments. That task was left to the gentlemanly Walter Burley Griffin, Wright's architectural assistant, who usually could resolve all difficulties. The Willits House is a massive cruciform

Above: The design of the Willits House is a palatial expression of the Prairie aesthetic, a rich massing of luxurious proportion.

Right: The tabletop roofline of the Willits House demonstrates a dramatic sense of grand proportion early in Wright's professional career.

structure with wings, four in all, extending from the central core—the great Roman brick chimney-core that on the interior provides for broad brick hearths throughout. A horizontal harmony is created by the use of low, hipped roofs.

On the first floor these long expansions of roof connect the sight lines that run from the first wing, containing a porte cochere (a covered side drive), entryway, and reception room on one side, with the dining room and porch extension on the opposite side of the house, wing three. Wing two contains the great living room with high windows and a walled terrace. The fourth wing is at the rear of the house and contains the kitchen and staff rooms. There is a powerful sense of lift to the structure as the house rises up to the second floor. The central wing of the house appears as a great cube, encrusted with tall, rich, art-glass windows that give the house a bejeweled rising sweep. These shimmering panes are set into long, narrow window

Above: Willits occupied the house until his death at the age of ninety-two. The building marks a significant point in Wright's career and represents the maturity of many of his ideas.

Left: The stucco walls give the house elegance and the rooflines add symmetry and grace.

frames on the first floor and on the second story become shortened rectangles across the expanse of the façade. Out of these windows, the full expanse of nature holds the house. Generous, sloping eaves with thin edges extend over the exterior of the entire house. String banding below the second-story sill line extends the horizontal expression of the house. The use of stucco across the outer surface of the house provides a crisp modernity, as well as practical plasticity that Wright used to full advantage in sculpting the exterior walls with dramatic flatness. At the front, low, stucco exterior walls box the terrace on the ground floor, providing both privacy and a furthering of the horizontal architectural framing. Wright introduced wide, classical urns at the corners of the terrace walls as elements to further solidify the symmetry. Ward Willits lived here until his death at ninety-two in 1951. Unlike other Wright patrons, his friendship did not survive Wright's ill treatment of his first wife, Catherine, or the unpaid loans Wright is said to have had with Willits.

E. ARTHUR DAVENPORT HOUSE

Address: 559 Ashland Avenue, River Forest, Illinois
Built: 1901

In the midst of the creation of many large, modern Prairie-style houses, Wright returned to a design that is semihistorical in this smaller, family-scaled house of E. Arthur Davenport. The house employed many features, however, that gave it a modern, Prairie character. The plan of the house, though more modest, is not so very different from the Willits House, a rectangular cruciform, with four arms extending from the central core. It was designed for Davenport, a man who would spend more than half a century working for George Pullman, the enigmatic president of the Pullman Company, the Chicago manufacturer of railroad sleeping cars. Unlike other Pullman workers, Davenport appears dispensed from the obligation of residing within the confines of "Pullman," the planned worker's city located on the far southern tip of Chicago. River Forest was a long way from Pullman in those days at the turn of the nineteenth century. Davenport and his wife, Susan, were very active in their bucolic River Forest community that already contained two of Wright's more radical home designs, the Williams House and the Winslow House. The design used here was more proportioned for the street.

Webster Tomlinson, Wright's architectural partner during this period and with whom he collaborated on the Henderson House, worked on this house with Wright. This is a house quite dissimilar from the massive Prairie residences Wright had been producing at

Left: The Davenport House in River Forest is designed in a cruciform, with exterior board-and-batten siding, art-glass windows, and broad, sweeping roof projections—all elements of the Prairie style.

this time. The angular, high-pitched, A-framed, gabled roof style is utilized in stark contrast to the low, hipped roof designs with which he was working, though it still offered the deep protective overhangs essential to the Prairie style.

The material used on the exterior is also a contrast to Wright's all-stucco preference in design. Here Wright returns to his tried-and-true board-and-batten horizontal cladding, reminiscent of the treatment used at the Goan House. These wooden boards help define the structure's horizontal sight lines and are continued up to the level of the roofline. The windows, however, add a more distinctive, historical feel, the Tudor/Elizabethan motif, and are generously used throughout the house. Aesthetically rich and textured, they are fashioned of long, narrow, rectangular glass panes in set lead, and are known as "ribbon windows" because they appear to weave themselves around the leading. When this house was first built, it had a front veranda with a sloping roof and a front window bay that was later removed. Someone in the Wright studio refashioned the exterior to its present design. Many feel that in its original design the house was probably the very image of the house Wright introduced in the *Ladies' Home Journal* magazine in July 1901. In two articles authored by Wright, he proposed his ultimate design for a domestic residence on a small scale, but roomy, for a modest sum. Because such a house was just what Americans were looking for, Wright became the focus of much attention.

Above: A Davenport House inglenook—a unique cozy, roomlike area built around a central hearth—has Wright-designed built-in benches and enormous Prairie-style fireplace irons.

Left: The interior of the Davenport House is filled with classical Wright furniture that completes the aesthetic of Wright's Prairie dwelling.

EDWARD C. WALLER GATES

Address: Auvergne Place, River Forest, Illinois
Built: 1901

All that is left of the vast Edward C. Waller estate—the house originally designed by Daniel Burnham, later remodeled by Wright, and the stables designed by Wright—are these stone gate pylons off busy Lake Street in the western Chicago suburb of River Forest, not far from the curving waters of the Des Plaines River. The house was demolished in 1939, but, the girth and depth of these stone works at the entry to that ghosted geography still, however, convey the dramatic significance of Waller's enterprise. The fresh appearance and modern simplicity of these gateways remain unblemished after a century. Restoration work has been both loving and painstaking. The recent addition of the square Prairie lanterns atop the pylons

Previous page and above: All that remains of the work done for Edward Waller by Wright are these gates. The lighting fixtures have recently been restored.

is a furthering of that restorative work at a place that was once the talk of Chicago. Edward C. Waller may very well have been Wright's most prestigious client and benefactor. After all, most of Wright's clients, though they were successful in their chosen fields, were usually not household names in either Chicago society or even within Chicago's bold world of business enterprise. Waller, however, was unique. He had been front and center for many significant moments of Chicago's growth and expansion.

Twenty years older than Wright, Waller was of that generation of impassioned American transplants who found Chicago a good place to make a fortune. So it is no accident that, like other savvy Chicagoan fortune seekers, Waller made his chink in Chicago's most responsive enterprise, real estate. A close friend of Chicago's most famous architect of the day, Daniel Burnham, Waller was at the center of many Chicago projects of note. He was the founder and president of the Central Safety Deposit Company that was responsible for the construction of William Le Baron Jenny's Home Insurance Company Building, the first steel framed skyscraper in America. Waller was also involved with the construction of the Rookery Building on LaSalle Street by Burnham and Root. It was no accident that Wright had an office in the building, as did the Luxfer Glass Company that played such a prominent role in many early Wright designs. Waller's company managed the Rookery and it is not hard to imagine Waller bringing Wright into Chicago's most glamorous downtown commercial structure as a tenant, or later ensuring his commission to remodel the famous building's atrium lobby. Waller was a great mentor to Wright. To say he was also his savior might not be too strong a characterization either. Given Wright's inability to maintain financial balance in his personal and professional life, Waller is one of the figures that repeatedly helped Wright to survive the terrors of his own making. Today, the entryway at Auvergne Place is still, however, the passage into one of Wright's other famous homes, the Winslow House. The iron gates themselves did not survive the ravages of time. The stone pylons stand, yet, as a Prairie memorial as much to Wright's relationship to Waller, as well as to the house and estate that once stood there.

1902

ARTHUR HEURTLEY HOUSE

Address: 318 Forest Avenue, Oak Park, Illinois
Built: 1902

Even on stately Forest Avenue, a street thick with Wright masterpieces, the square-plan Prairie-style Heurtley House stands out, bold with a modernity that is fresh and visually appealing. Its

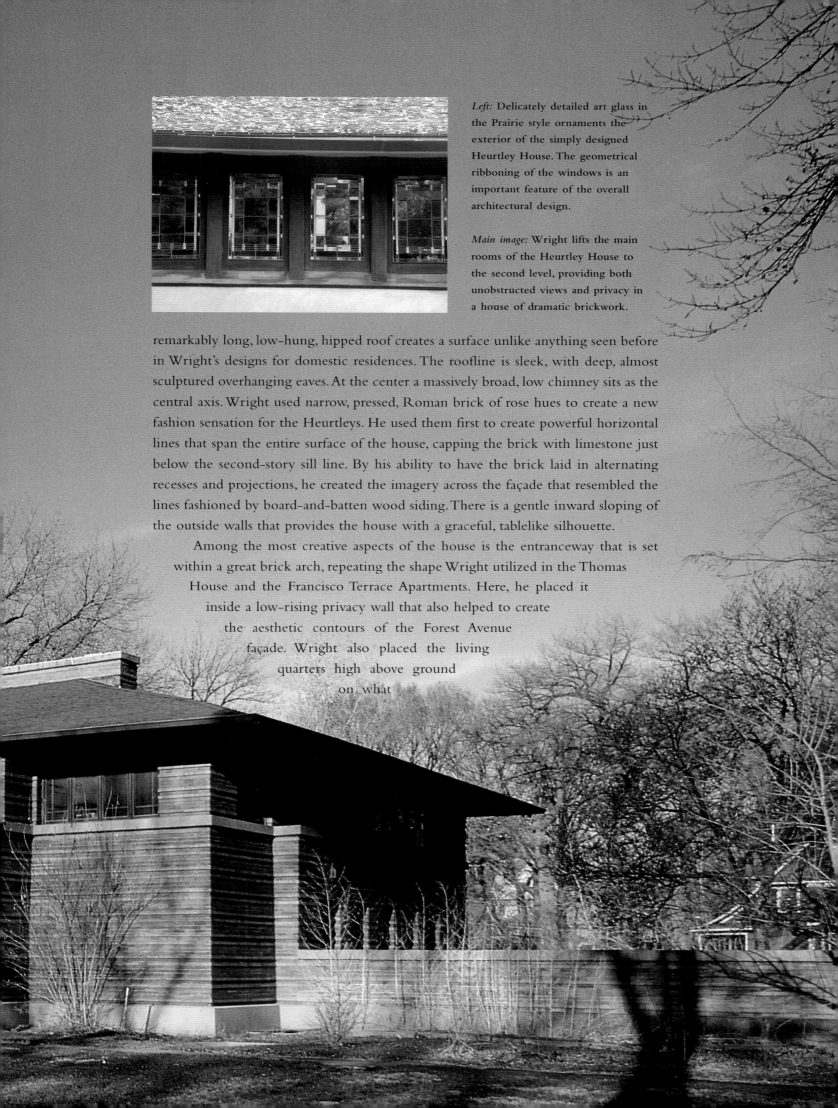

Left: Delicately detailed art glass in the Prairie style ornaments the exterior of the simply designed Heurtley House. The geometrical ribboning of the windows is an important feature of the overall architectural design.

Main image: Wright lifts the main rooms of the Heurtley House to the second level, providing both unobstructed views and privacy in a house of dramatic brickwork.

remarkably long, low-hung, hipped roof creates a surface unlike anything seen before in Wright's designs for domestic residences. The roofline is sleek, with deep, almost sculptured overhanging eaves. At the center a massively broad, low chimney sits as the central axis. Wright used narrow, pressed, Roman brick of rose hues to create a new fashion sensation for the Heurtleys. He used them first to create powerful horizontal lines that span the entire surface of the house, capping the brick with limestone just below the second-story sill line. By his ability to have the brick laid in alternating recesses and projections, he created the imagery across the façade that resembled the lines fashioned by board-and-batten wood siding. There is a gentle inward sloping of the outside walls that provides the house with a graceful, tablelike silhouette.

Among the most creative aspects of the house is the entranceway that is set within a great brick arch, repeating the shape Wright utilized in the Thomas House and the Francisco Terrace Apartments. Here, he placed it inside a low-rising privacy wall that also helped to create the aesthetic contours of the Forest Avenue façade. Wright also placed the living quarters high above ground on what normally would be considered the second floor. He already proved how successful this could be at the Thomas House and Henderson House, although here it appears that the elevation is heightened. An open floor plan permits a continuous flow across the family rooms of the living area. There is no break between the dining room and small breakfast nook at the north end that continues through the living room at the center of the house, all the way to the enclosed porch at the south end. At the back portion of this upper level of the house are the three bedrooms, as well as the kitchen.

This open floor plan was welcomed by the Heurtleys, who are said to have been very social individuals with a gift for entertaining. Arthur Heurtley was a young man of forty-two when he commissioned Wright to build his most extraordinary house. Though he had been born in Boston, he had lived in Chicago in the days before the Great Fire of 1871. He was a successful Chicago banker and an officer of the Northern Trust Bank from its founding. He had the distinction of bringing to the bank some of the business interests of the Chicago retail tycoon Marshall Field. In

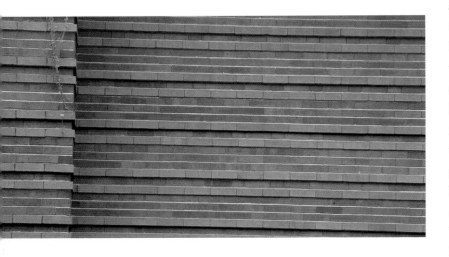

addition to playing golf at the Oak Park Country Club and tennis at the River Forest Tennis Club, whose clubhouse was designed by Wright, Heurtley was an avid man of music who filled his home with bright sounds and lyrical rhythms as fresh as the great house in which he lived. Recent restoration has given the house the unequaled exterior beauty with which Wright originally endowed it. Heurtley also commissioned Wright to remodel his summer house in Michigan's Upper Peninsula.

Above: Detail of intricate brickwork ribbing on the façade allows the house to have a strong horizontal character reminiscent of rough board-and-batten cladding.

Below: The extensive projections of the Heurtley House roof provide a valuable level of shelter, particularly on the upper-level outdoor veranda.

Right: Wright's inclusion of a low-rise front wall provides privacy for the entryway that is hidden from the street.

WILLIAM E. MARTIN HOUSE

Address: 636 N. East Avenue, Oak Park, Illinois
Built: 1902

There is little dispute that the William E. Martin House is one of the greatest houses of the Prairie era. Its size and aristocratic lift single it out as one of Wright's most dynamic renderings from the period of his most innovative Prairie expression. The house also contains one of Wright's finest interiors filled with specialty furniture of Prairie design. It has one of Wright's most successful "cave" interiors, as his cozy, hearth-centered family rooms have become known. In many ways, the house was as fantastic as the man who commissioned it. William E. Martin and his brother Darwin D. Martin were not only responsible for Wright's eventual design and building of some seven other buildings, but they, like others before them, would become patrons of the ubiquitous Wright. Like many other Wright clients, William E. Martin was not only a successful man of business as a partner in the E-Z Stove and Shoe Polish Factory in Chicago (a building designed by Wright), but also an imaginative inventor. Martin held a patent for one of the earliest applications of the color labeling process on tin cans, in addition to another one for the design of an early traffic-control signal system. Like Wright's first independent client,

Above: **Wright achieves an unprecedented visual beauty in the Martin House, his last three-story Prairie residence.**

William Herman Winslow, William Martin was an early enthusiast of the steam-driven automobile, sporting his own Stanley Steamer.

It is said that Martin and his brother were motoring one day and saw Wright's Oak Park Home and Studio. Its design so captivated them that they knocked on Wright's door. By the time they left, William Martin had commissioned the house. This was to be Wright's last three-story Prairie house. Wright appeared to be experimenting with both vertical sweep and horizontal expansion here. Both dimensions ultimately produced a house of unusual Prairie grandeur whose vertical rise is accentuated by the curious proportions of its three levels, the third of which is specially scaled for use by children. At both the second and first levels, gracefully pitched, low-hung, hipped roofs with deep sloping eaves seem as if they are cascading, floor by floor, like an architectural waterfall. At the ground level, a long roof flows across the south end of the house over a veranda that is an extension of the dining room, with a flair similar to the design used in the Willits House. Wright took full advantage of the expansive Oak Park lot by setting

Above: The plaster and wood trim of this three-story dwelling is reminiscent of the Fricke residence, but is closer to the Prairie ideal.

Above: The leading, or caming, of Wright's ornamental windows reach a delicate, Prairie richness of proportion in the Martin House that expands the beauty of exterior stucco and wood detail.

the house up against the extreme north end of the lot line and expanding out in a dramatic visual sweep. This also provided Wright with the space necessary to include a spacious garden in his design. Later a pergola was built that was the center of garden life. Sadly, it was later demolished. It is a curious fact that W. E. Martin and his wife made visits to five of Wright's Oak Park houses, conducting their own practical investigation of Wright's work. "You never witnessed such enthusiasm," he wrote his brother. "No one will admit a fault in their house."

Above: The exterior stucco cladding of the Martin House became a high achievement in Wright's ever-growing ability to fashion graceful contours and proportioned surfaces.

1903

J. J. WALSER HOUSE

Address: 42 North Central Avenue, Chicago, Illinois
Built: 1903

It is often said that Frank Lloyd Wright's structures are solid, tough, and more resilient than they might look at first glance. Nothing reinforces this more sadly than when a Wright building is under the wrecking ball, to the dismayed efforts of the wreckers. The sturdiness of Wright's designs is especially evident at the Walser House. The house was designed for Jacob Walser, one of Wright's most affluent clients, a man much admired by the architect. He reserved only the highest regard for Walser, who, like Edward Waller, had only a high school education. However, these men were carried by character and values of a higher refinement. Wright said they were men of "unspoiled instincts and untainted ideals."

The Walser House recently celebrated its hundredth anniversary. Despite the ravages of time and urban wear, the house still retains a genteel beauty, as well as all the telltale elements that designate this as one of Wright's signature Prairie-style dwellings. This is a true urban house located in the western Chicago neighborhood of Austin, abutting Oak Park. Long ago, the community underwent an urban transition that left it thick with large apartment buildings, two of which sandwich this weary residence. The result, today, is that this large, handsome house appears smaller than it should if it had more space on which to sit. But that aesthetic concern is the least of this house's worries. Further urban decay and years of neglect have seriously distressed this jewel, though the grandeur of Wright's artistry is still apparent in this Chicago landmark and close inspection reveals certain key Wright characteristics are still intact.

The yellowish all-stucco exterior has the look of old parchment, and thus accrues an almost Elizabethan patina, though such a revivalist attribute of design was never intentional in Wright's plan. There is, however, a very definite Tudor feeling to the heavily worn façade. The cypress stripping trim and window frames give off a "half-timbered" quality. The wood trim is in desperate need of restaining and repair, but its dark finish is still thick in places. Like Wright's other Prairie masterpieces, the Walser House is a cruciform-plan structure, a central two-story core with north and

Above and right: The Prairie character of the Walser House is expressed in its deep, overhanging eaves, stucco and wood exterior cladding, and cruciform plan.

south arms projecting out across the house's first floor. Wright introduced an open floor plan to the interior here for Walser in which the entire first level is treated as a single room. From the front living room to back dining room, an open flow enables easy movement, a radical idea in 1903. The entrance is located on the north side of the house, concealed from the street. A generous overhang along the lower-floor roofline provides shelter at the entranceway. Five bedrooms and one bath are located on the second level. Deep, overhanging eaves projecting from the second-story hipped roof establish a familiar Wright Prairie feature. This is a house designed with many expansive sets of rectangular wood-framed windows across the face and the sides. Once, they were bejeweled with sparkling art glass. Sadly, this glass has been extracted and subsequently sold. A central chimney block, wide, massive, and sleek, forms an important Prairie axis that is both aesthetic and utilitarian. A full basement contains storage space, as well as the heating apparatus, coalbunker, and laundry facilities.

Above: The cruciform arm of the Walser House adds important horizontal sight lines from the wing's flat roof, horizontal banding, and window leading.

Right: The rear of the Walser House shows the deep-set overhang and the ribboning of upper-level banding.

EDWIN H. CHENEY HOUSE

Address: 520 N. East Avenue, Oak Park, Illinois
Built: 1903

This remarkable two-story, Roman-brick bungalow has an impressive architectural pedigree. Wright achieved handsome aesthetic proportions with the narrow, pressed brick that he had used so effectively in his house for Arthur Heurtley. But this house will probably live forever as the house that brought Wright into the lives of electrical engineer Edwin H. Cheney and his erudite wife, Mamah Borthwick Cheney, the woman who would help Wright alter both his professional and personal life. The house at first glance is deceptive, looking like a simple, one-story bungalow. In reality, though, it is, in fact, a two-story structure whose main story is lifted a full story above a raised basement, concealed to the eye on the street by a walled terrace. Wright introduced a further expression of his "open floor" design for the Cheneys in the interior. The main rooms—living room, dining room, and library—all flow into one another, a new concept in modern living and a design technique that was fresh and exciting. The open plan begins to reduce the architectural dependency on the typical series of familiar rooms structured like independent boxes. A kitchen, four bedrooms, and two baths complete Wright's interior plan. In the full lower-level basement, Wright placed more bedrooms and a bath, as well as a billiard room.

Above: **The low, rising roof has wide horizontal dimensions, a notable feature of Wright's Prairie style.**

Right: **Proportion and symmetry are strong and important features of the Cheney House, which has an Asian aesthetic influence in the simplicity of its profile.**

The exterior of the house was originally designed to include a series of ten-foot-high Roman brick walls that provided more privacy, as well as large amounts of concealed outdoor space. A portion of this wall was removed during a modern restoration to some fire-damaged portions of the house. One large, low-pitched hipped roof with deep, overhanging eaves establishes the exterior angular sweep of the house. Wright anchored the house at its center with a great central chimney. For the Cheneys, he went further by being able to use a portion of the space behind this chimney to introduce a hidden skylight to carry light to a portion of the unused attic space. The main entrance to the house was imaginatively concealed by Wright and requires some effort to reach through a series of turns along the garden pathway that eventually ends at a series of steps to a small entry. Above the line of the wall, the windows of the main

Above: The dining room of the Cheney House is expressive of the Prairie elegance Wright insisted on in his houses. Chairs add to the Wrightian geometric aesthetic beneath the timbered ceiling and are surrounded by built-in furniture exact to the architect's specification.

Right top: The Cheney House living room is anchored by the large hearth of handsome Roman brick and the warmth created by the rich wood textures.

Right bottom: Ceiling beams are utilized to enhance the Prairie design, as is the backlit, art-glass window in this lower-floor bedroom.

floor of the Cheney House are richly encrusted with sparkling art glass—all fifty-two of them. The house is deceptively high, appearing to ride close to the earth with a surprising kindred tie to the great primitive Celtic monolith and settlement at Newgrange in Ireland. Edwin Cheney remained at this house with his children after his wife ran off with Wright in 1909. He stayed here even after his children and their mother were tragically murdered in 1914. He finally left in 1926, moving to St. Louis, having remarried some years earlier. Today, the house, fashioned with such interior greatness by Wright, is operated as an Oak Park bed and breakfast.

THE ABRAHAM LINCOLN CENTER

Address: 700 East Oakwood Boulevard, Chicago, Illinois

Built: 1903

This curious building on Chicago's South Side, not far from the present campus of the Illinois Institute of Technology, has its roots in Wright's mother's family and is somewhat a collaboration between Wright and the Chicago architect Dwight Perkins. Wright's uncle, the Reverend Jenkin Lloyd Jones, was a Unitarian pastor at All Saints Church in Chicago. Wright lived in this Chicago neighborhood after first coming to the city. He and Perkins were both church members. It was also the church in which Wright first met Catherine Tobin, his first wife. Following a stormy conflict within his religious organization, Jones and all his parishioners left the Unitarian communion and established a separate, independent church. The temper of this schism was totally in keeping with Jenkin Lloyd Jones's blustery, unpredictable character. Joseph Silsbee, the Chicago architect who first employed Wright in Chicago, had previously designed Jones's Chicago All Saints Church (now demolished) that was located directly across the street from the Abraham Lincoln Center.

Following his break with the Unitarians, Jones asked his nephew to design the new church facility. Because they were to have no official sectarian affiliation with any church, the new center to be built would be named for the sixteenth president of the United States. Architecturally, it was to embody the independence and unfettered restraints that characterized Jones's new Chicago mission. Jones stipulated that the exterior of the building was to resemble an ordinary Chicago commercial office building. He was not looking for ecclesiastical architecture. Wright found working with his uncle an onerous undertaking. They had many disagreements during the building of the center. Perkins, a cousin of Wright's studio assistant, Marion Mahony, attempted to promote harmony by taking charge of the supervision of the construction. He, too, found Jones a hard man to deal with. Perkins soon abandoned the project, like Wright, leaving the words "bldg. completed over protest of architect," written in red crayon on the final set of plans.

Right: The Abraham Lincoln Center was Jenkin Lloyd Jones's second Chicago church and was constructed as a multiuse facility to generate income for his independent church.

The design of the Abraham Lincoln Center had endless junctures at which Wright and his uncle could quarrel, so complete was the structure with the industrious design features requested by Reverend Jenkin Lloyd Jones. To start with, there was the whole concept of the building's multipurpose function. In addition to the necessity of a large, two-story auditorium and assembly halls to serve the needs of worshippers, plans included meeting rooms, gymnasiums, kitchens, and a residential apartment for Jones and his family. In addition, the plan called for the inclusion of rental retail facilities that were expected to be an added source of income for the church. This was a revolutionary idea in 1903, one Wright would have had firsthand experience with while at the firm of Adler and Sullivan. Their Auditorium Theater Building of 1887 employed a similar blending of a hotel, opera house, and retail tenants in a startlingly modern multiuse facility. The Abraham Lincoln Center, mostly devoid of any telltale Wright design features, does include the architect's rectangular openness and interior brickwork inside the two-story auditorium. Within this meeting space are included horizontally rectangular windows on both the first and second levels, a style Wright would soon employ at his most celebrated church, the Unity Temple in Oak Park. Though a building on a modest scale, it has a very modern crispness to its façade. Its eight floors of expansive exterior brickwork are a prefigurement of the industrial exterior artistry Wright later used at the E–Z Shine Polish factory. The Abraham Lincoln Center's brick massing and window design has a more haunting touch of Wright than might seem at first glance. Little attention, however, is given to this building as a Wright-designated structure. But his shadow is here, unmistakably. A renovation during the 1970s has strengthened the building's endurance.

Right: An aerial view of Wright's Abraham Lincoln Center, showing its office capacity and the symmetry of its design.

THE SCOVILLE PARK FOUNTAIN

Address: Lake Street at Oak Park Avenue,
Oak Park, Illinois
Built: 1903

When Wright first designed this Oak Park fountain with Richard Bock for the Horse Show Association of Oak Park, horses were a familiar conveyance along the cobbles of the leafy suburb. The stone fountain tablature is reminiscent of an ancient Celtic dolmen. The square opening within the rectangular body of the fountain is topped by another measured rectangular slab. The fountain is adorned with harmonious carvings on the interior square slab near the

water trough itself, as well as on the exterior portions of the façade and the lintel. Beyond the utility of the fountain that was designed for easy access for both humans and horses, it is an exercise in Wright's fascination with simple shapes. There is nothing ostensibly complex about this structure that recalls the tall sculpturing of a Wright Prairie residence not unlike the Henderson House or the nearby Martin House. A further link to other commissions was the fact that the inventor, Charles E. Roberts, for whom Wright had remodeled the Burnham House and Stable, was a member of the committee responsible for commissioning the fountain. Roberts was also head of the committee to select an architect to design the Unity Temple in Oak Park. The fountain is a reminder, in a scale of remarkable proportion, of his patronage to Wright in things great and simple. Wright's collaboration with the sculptor Richard Bock has a decidedly modern provenance, one that gives him the lion's share of the credit for this fountain dedicated on July 24, 1909. Wright appears to have had a much earlier hand in its design in 1903. This is by no means the original fountain that was

located some hundred feet east of this spot. The fountain was actually replaced in 1969 to commemorate the centennial of Wright's birth that he vainly and inaccurately held to make him seem two years younger than he really was.

Above: This concrete relief identifies the fact that the fountain was restored for the 1969 "centenary" of Wright's birth, which turned out to be two years out of date—a result of Wright's earlier stretching of the facts of his 1867 birth.

Right: The interior relief memorializes the relationship between people and animals.

Above: The Scoville Park Fountain has the form and shape of a Celtic dolmen with rectangular slabs and tablelike lintels.

1904

MRS. THOMAS H. GALE
HOUSE

Address: 6 Elizabeth Court,
Oak Park, Illinois
Built: 1904

Using the date on the perspective drawing as evidence, the design for this house dates from 1904 or earlier. The commonly accepted date of 1909 is that of construction. Thomas Gale is familiar to Wright students as the Oak Park Realtor who built two Wright homes on Chicago Avenue in 1892. Laura R. Gale was a widow when this dramatically cantilevered house was completed for herself and her children, following her husband's death in 1907. Here, Wright created one of his most distinctive designs anywhere, and many see in the stirring, bold, extensive cantilevering of the roof and balcony a prefiguring of the architect's radical design for Fallingwater, the "waterfall house" he built in 1938 for Edgar J. Kaufmann in Mill Run, Pennsylvania.

The Gale House sits up on a gentle rise on a winding street of historical and colorful houses that look for all the world like a Hollywood streetscape. But it is Mrs. Gale's house that alters the local terrain among the gingerbread Victorians and the clapboard Queen Annes. A spaceship could be no less startling on this cozy Oak Park street. What a ruckus it must have ignited in 1909 can only be guessed at. This is Wright at his most astounding, pushing the edges of revolutionary design by the application of simplicity and understated elegance. Most of the significant details of the house were completed when Wright left Oak Park for Europe in 1909. Herman Von Holst, his most able assistant, was given the responsibility for completing the project. The house rests at a slight angle in relation to its elevated property, with the result that it permits the sweeping, cantilevered projections to be seen in a gentle profile. In addition, this angularity thrusts the house into a natural frame created by two soaring oak trees. No one passing the house can fail to be engaged by the expansive tablature of the roof. Once

Right: **Wright's placement of the Mrs. Thomas Gale House on the incline of a small hill sets the structure into an intimate relationship with nature, fulfilling his ideas of organic architectural design.**

again, the design reflects the Celtic aesthetic of the table dolmens so familiar to Wright's Welsh ancestors.

The roofs are not only aesthetic, but they have a practical application as well, providing wide shelter over both exterior balconies. For this Prairie masterpiece, the architect used his premier exterior cladding, stucco and wood, to enhance the flat surfaces of the exterior with graceful precision. It is thought that Wright had originally wanted to use concrete for the exterior following his success at Unity Temple. The house also has the cubical geometry seen in his "Fireproof House for $5,000," though the dramatic projections of the cantilevering alters the similarity of the façades. At the side of the house, windows have smaller cantilevered projections above that further extend the sense of shelter from both sun and weather. Balconies

Above: Window sets and horizontal banding contrast with the sculptured stucco of the Mrs. Thomas Gale House.

are broad and expansive, creating further living space extended into the nature that abounds. The main entry is hidden from the perspective of the street, being set on the left side of the house, tucked behind the vertical massing of the façade. It is reminiscent of the hidden door at the Adams House in Highland Park. On the interior of the first floor, Wright provided the widow Gale with an open floor plan that freed interior space, with the living room opening to the other areas. The dining room is to the rear. The house underwent a series of renovations in each of the past three decades. The exterior stucco is presently painted in a very earthy terra cotta that adds a fresh, vibrant cache to a dwelling excitingly ahead of its time and that fits well into the present.

Above: **Stucco becomes a fluid sculptural substance in Wright's amazing architectural design, never more profound than in the cantilevered geometry of the Mrs. Thomas Gale House.**

UNITY TEMPLE

Address: 875 Lake Street, Oak Park, Illinois
Built: 1904

The architectural significance of this startling church takes on added importance against Wright's previously frustrated efforts at church design for his uncle, the Reverend Jenkin Lloyd Jones, just the year before. Wright's project has added irony considering Jones and his entire parish community left the Unitarian communion to begin their own independent church. But all this really pales in the face of the revolutionary structure that Wright was ultimately able to design for the Oak Park Unitarian community, following the destruction of their former home by fire. Wright's new church complex served not only their utilitarian purposes, but it was an opportunity for his unique American aesthetic to fashion a piece of ecclesiastical architecture that was fresh, bold, and modern. Wright's Unity Temple may be the most original and modern form of church architecture in America. Its form seemed to rise out of the very prairie on which it sat. Its unbridled modernity was a challenge to the very tastes and the sensibilities of everyone in the age of President Theodore Roosevelt. It continues right up to the present.

At the Unity Temple, formed entirely of poured concrete, Wright introduced a substance with which he would sculpt a worship center into a sophisticated cube and reflect an age in modern art that was erupting on the aesthetical horizon. At Unity Temple, Wright reached for his most perfect geometric form, the cube, and breathed into it a radically new American architectural form. The structure of the Unity Temple (as the whole complex is now called) is actually two cubes, one large (originally called Unity Temple), suiting the worship needs of the community, and the other, called Unity House, designed on a smaller scale, connected to the larger by an entryway and reception area that serves as a bridge. The effect created by these two cubes and the central passage forms the remarkable expansive horizontal character of the overall structural plan. Broad, flat, overhanging roof plateaus, familiar from the great sweeping Prairie houses Wright had already built, added to the powerful modern architectural freedom with which Unity Temple was imbued. Wright was able to achieve in the poured concrete a similar elasticity that he had

Right: **The tall modernity of Unity Temple remains one of Wright's most readily identifiable designs in America. Formed of poured concrete, Wright sculptured the building into being and set in motion a new, defining architectural imperative for his life.**

Right: The interior of the Unity Temple continues Wright's expansive Prairie aesthetic displayed in the ceiling lamps, furniture, and embellishments such as the long, narrow, symmetrical spindles.

Above: The architect believed concrete to be the perfect substance for exterior cladding, capable of remarkable elasticity.

discovered in his use of stucco in domestic design. With it, he was able to achieve a remarkably flat surface sweep throughout the large areas of external wall space of the façade of the building.

Upon that sense of stylish lift, he introduced a decorative series of columns just beneath the deep overhangs. On the columns themselves, he applied one of his earliest uses of Mayan decorative motifs. These graceful cubist design forms derived from ancient Mexican cultural traditions served the scope of the Unity Temple well. In some ways the entire project was evocative of that simple, cubist primitive design mode—the upward vertical projections giving a dramatic visual lift not unlike the pre-Columbian pyramids and temples of the Mayans. While the exterior of the Unity Temple was revolutionary, the true aesthetical revolution was taking place on the interior. There, Wright created a sense of space that was both rich and radical.

With the Prairie motif, he induced a new sense of interior space, open and free, that was of the most dramatically radical architectural nature. Wright himself used to delight in saying that what he had actually designed here was the open space itself, so bold was his whole new concept in architecture. In

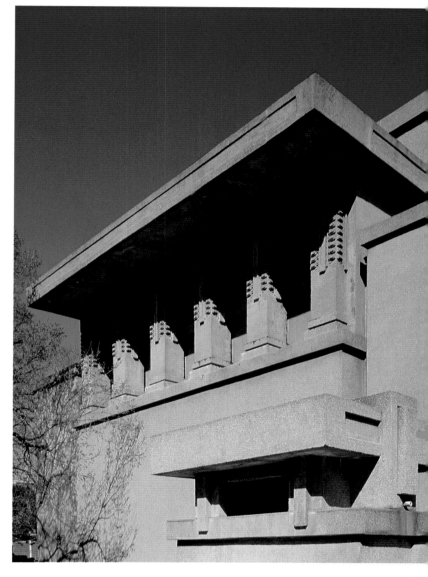

Above: The dramatic cantilevering of Unity Temple is deepened by the fact that it is fashioned from concrete. Wright embellished the structure to a geometric ornamentation that is both simple and primitive, a design element he would repeat with fresh passion in his work in the 1920s.

the upper reaches of the worship center, bejeweled art glass expressing the cubist Prairie theme brought light into the interior in a most sensational manner. Everything from the light fixtures, furniture, and wainscoting to the intricate skylights carried the message of Prairie modernity. Panoramas of the exterior demonstrated the elegance and vibrancy of a new art form that even the most conservative members of the Unitarian church recognized as the beginning of another age. The design is both monolithic and otherworldly, evoking both the massive artistic achievements of past civilizations and a new age of architecture in America. Scale, proportion, and balance are so effectively used here that they speak a language so powerful as to instantly seize the viewer. This was one of Wright's personal favorites after a lifetime of architectural achievements.

1905

HIRAM BALDWIN HOUSE

Address: 205 South Essex Road,
Kenilworth, Illinois
Built: 1905

The Hiram Baldwin House is another house that Wright turned over to his assistant to complete following his departure for Europe with his mistress, Mamah Borthwick Cheney. One of Wright's more noble Prairie-style homes, it sits in the refined aristocracy of the village of Kenilworth, an unusually planned suburban community along the bluffs of Lake Michigan, sixteen miles north of downtown Chicago. Sandwiched between the communities of Wilmette and Winnetka, this small enclave was the idea of Chicago businessman Joseph Sears, a partner of N. K. Fairbanks, a noted Chicago businessman.

Sears conceived of a country community of child-focused families not far from downtown. With just 300 people, he incorporated that vision in 1896, galvanized by spacious properties built with only the highest quality of construction. The village is an Arts and Crafts wonder, reflecting that style in its fountains, town posts, and homes. So well planned was this community that Jens Jensen, America's foremost garden landscape designer, fashioned the botanicals, while architects like Daniel Burnham and George Washington Maher created stately homes. All streets run northeast and southwest to ensure that every window of every house has sun at some point during the day. This was a village of high ideals and noble purposes, a place to which the tired, successful man of commerce could return at night to be revived by his family.

Into this remarkable paradigm of aesthetics, Hiram Baldwin commissioned Wright to produce a Prairie manse, an architectural masterpiece that reflected the high sense of hearth and home so cherished in Kenilworth. Wright produced a handsome stucco and wood-trimmed house of sweeping horizontal character. On the interior, the living room is connected to a graceful semicircular bay,

Right: **Wright's sophisticated horizontal Prairie form has a strong architectural profile in the Baldwin House. Wright has concealed the front door in a recessed side entryway not visible from the street.**

Above: Stucco cladding is given a deeply expanded horizontal character by the application of architectural banding and the deep sheltering projection of cantilevered overhangs.

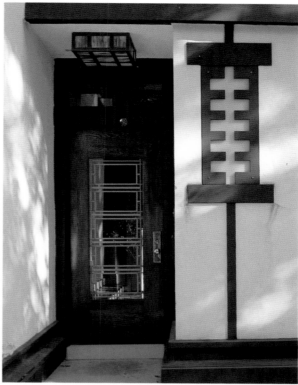

Above: Large, geometrically square window panes fill the interior of the Baldwin House with an abundance of natural light, as well as permitting an intimacy with nature on the exterior.

Above: The entrance to the Baldwin House is concealed by being tucked away perpendicular to the street and recessed into its own entry structure.

while the central hearth sets the axis of the structure connecting the dining room, reception room, and enclosed porch. On the second level, Wright indulges in dramatic cantilevering in the bedrooms at each end of the house projecting out over the first floor, as he does in the Kibben Ingalls House of this same period. The grand master bedroom has its own hearth.

Windows are geometric squares with strong mullions familiar from Wright's usage in the Evans House. The hipped roof has a gentle slope and extensive projecting eaves at each end. The roofline helps to deepen the sense of the horizontal line. The house was originally built with an abundance of fine art glass that has since been removed. The inclusion of Wright's Prairie style in the acceptable architectural design modes in Kenilworth was significant and only a decade removed from the days when his early Prairie design was considered quite radical. The style was ready-made for the Arts and Crafts style so cherished in this tiny community that to this day remains a hidden village of deep prosperity and refinement. It ranks forty-fourth out of 250 of America's wealthiest communities and still has fewer than 800 households.

MARY M. W. ADAMS HOUSE

Address: 1923 Lake Avenue, Highland Park, Illinois
Built: 1905

Mary Adams has the distinction of being Wright's oldest client. Born in 1835, she was seventy years old when she took possession of her sprawling Prairie residence in Highland Park, then a burgeoning suburban town along the Lake Michigan shoreline thirty-five miles north of Chicago. The thirty-minute commute by rail made this an ideal community for Chicago's commercial barons. It was the town where Wright built Ward Willits's Prairie masterpiece. Today, it is thick with the work of many of Wright's students and studio assistants, as well as other first-rate Chicago architects from Barry Byrne and John Van Bergen to David Adler, William Deknatel, and Howard Van Doren Shaw. For many years its Ravinia Casino has been the summer home of the Chicago Symphony Orchestra. Jens Jensen, America's greatest landscape architect, had his studio here and influenced the local shape of flora. The town is affluent and artsy.

Wright's Adams House predates most of the expansion of good architecture. Given her age, it might seem remarkable that Mary Adams should have turned to Wright for the design of a new home in the early days of the twentieth century. No record affords the opportunity to know the details of their meeting. But as she was a member of the Christian Science church, her independence and individualism seem a familiar draw to Wright's work, as it did another member of that church, the inventor William E. Martin of Oak Park. A Christian Science Society was established in Highland Park as early as 1899 by two women seeking relief from illness, and within a matter of months, four women were enrolled in meetings, although it is not recorded if Mary Adams was among them. Given her age, it might be safe to assume she was a charter member. The Christian Science church opened in Highland Park in 1905, the very same year Mary Adams's house was built by Wright. This is an example of Wright's "developing" Prairie concept. Some have suggested that the Adams House was a prototype of "A Fireproof House for $5,000." This was the square-planned dwelling that first appeared in the April 1907 issue of *Ladies' Home Journal* and in which Wright demonstrated a classic but modest modern American home. The suggestion would make the Adams House a distant relative of the Hunt House in LaGrange (1907) and the Stockman House in Mason City, Iowa (1908). Wright's design here umbrellas the house with expansive, deep, overhanging eaves that gracefully provide

both shelter for the stucco walls and artistic beauty through their Prairie aesthetic. It is the roofs that establish the dramatic horizontal line, so essential here in the Prairie ethos. The entrance is tucked into the sheltered entry passage just at the side of the front porch that is now enclosed. A broad and spacious hipped roof extends over the porch from which Mary Adams could easily summon members of her household staff via an inventive internal call network. An open-sided, Roman-brick hearth in the living room extends into the porch area. Wright enhanced the dining room at the far side of the house with an expansive series of windows that afforded Mary Adams extensive panoramas. Sadly, she would only have three years in the house before her death. In many ways it was a house that Wright built around her and the needs of her final years—an economical house, easily built.

Above: The Mary M. W. Adams House is an expansive Prairie-style dwelling with overhangs that add drama and practical utility protecting the stucco cladding from climatic assault.

WILLIAM A. GLASNER HOUSE

Address: 850 Sheridan Road, Glencoe, Illinois
Built: 1905

Glencoe is a North Shore Chicago suburb of craggy ravines and deeply forested residential neighborhoods along the waters of Lake Michigan. In 1905, it was the kind of terrain that was appealing to Frank Lloyd Wright, from which he liked to see his architecture rise. The Glasner House is best understood against the background of the times. It was built on the edge of a ravine and was designed as a utilitarian residence in which people could live without the necessity of servants. While that might seem strange to modern ears, it was a revolutionary concept for anyone in the upper-middle class of 1905. Keeping house was heavy work and few who could afford it did so without the assistance of someone to help with the daily routines of life. Before the coming of most of the technology many people take for granted today, servants were both inexpensive and a necessity for many, particularly those who lived in large Victorian houses that required constant upkeep. Here in the Glasner House, Wright tried his hand at a domestic dwelling that would liberate the homeowner from the need for having live-in help. This was more of a revolutionary idea than you might think at first glance. It meant that a living space would have to be created that shaped itself to a new form of utility and practicality. Wright sought to accomplish this first with a structure that had only one story. Many see this as a prefigurement of his later, post–World War II style known as "Usonian."

For Glasner, Wright built a simplified house. The entrance led directly to the living room that was just off the kitchen. The space provided no separate area for dining. An economy of space is the optimum beginning for practical living. The low-hung, hipped roof has extensive overhanging eaves that provide the house with both practical shelter and aesthetic style. The format, or plan, of the house calls for one long wing projecting into a shorter, perpendicular wing at the rear of the structure. The original design incorporated two octagonal spaces, similar to the one in Wright's own studio in Oak Park and the Bagley House in Hinsdale. Here, one connected to the living room was to serve as a library; the other, off the bedroom, was to serve as a sewing room. The house is compact and practical, devoid of the unnecessary details that complicate everyday living. Wright returned to a very practical element for the exterior rough-sawn, board-and-batten cladding that wears well and requires little attention from the homeowner. He used it elsewhere in the Henry Wallis Cottage and the Charles S. Ross House, both in Wisconsin, with great success. Wright artfully filled the windows with handsome jeweled glass that filtered a glittering light throughout the house. This house was an important experiment in practicality, a byword of the modern age that was at the horizon.

Left: Extravagant cantilevering allowed Wright to create dramatically projecting rooftops at the William A. Glasner House with eaves of wide, sheltering reach. The exterior cladding is board-and-batten, significantly American and a favorite of the architect's.

CHARLES E. BROWN HOUSE

Address: 2420 Harrison Street, Evanston, Illinois
Built: 1905

This house sits in the North Shore suburb of Evanston, the home of Northwestern University. The Lake Michigan shoreline forms the eastern border of this tony municipality whose character is that of a small, prosperous metropolis. There are many points of parallel with Oak Park—the independent liberal consciousness of its citizens, its artsy, commercial expression of quiet success, and the abundance of tasteful, baronial residential architecture. Just to the west of the university campus is this handsome Wright house designed for Charles A. Brown, a man who most likely was a real estate developer in the early decades of the twentieth century, and who built this house as an experiment for others of similar style. Mr. Brown is said to have never occupied the house.

But despite its curious pedigree, in true Wright style, this house is an eye-catcher, for it displays many familiar design motifs found in other Wright Prairie-style houses. No element is more demonstrative and evocative of Wright than the expansive, cantilevered roof that sweeps across twenty-two feet of the exterior veranda. With a depth of almost ten feet, this roof projects with an almost gravity-defying grandeur from the façade. It creates a demonstrative façade projection that Wright used with even more grandeur at the J. Kibben Ingalls House just four years later in River Forest. Both this cantilevered projection and the main roof of the Brown House

Right: The expansive cantilevering of the Charles Brown House seems to defy gravity and provides a deep sheltering by the roof projections. Exterior board-and-batten cladding marks a return by Wright to one of his favorite Prairie design features.

are hipped roof designs. The exterior cladding, horizontal board-and-batten, is a return to a familiar Wright characteristic, one that he uses with less frequency in this period of Prairie grandeur. It provides the house with its defining horizontal Prairie character, a design element that is also extended by the four square-framed, double-paned, narrow, horizontal windows that extend beneath the overhang across the façade of the second story. That narrow, rectangular geometric shape is repeated between the windows in a raised, decorative embellishment. Together with the banding at the roof edge, the further thin banding above the windows and the corner wraparound banding, the house has the exterior flavor of the William Adams House on a much less dramatic scale.

The interior of the house also echoes Wright's architectural voice with the application of rich art-glass leaded windows that permit maximum light to fill the public space. An expansive living room stretches across the full width of the house with a hearth of narrow Roman brick acting as an anchor of interior domestic life. The rear of the house contains the dining room and the kitchen. Four bedrooms and a bath are located on the second floor. It is possible that Wright was experimenting with this design module in 1905, which prefigures his American Systems-built designs just before World War I. This is a more robust and dramatic dwelling than his Systems-built efforts, in which his willingness to provide a family home of uncomplicated utility and a modest price lacks the flourish of his exterior drama. This house may be a prototype, but it certainly is a sturdy domestic dwelling in which the fingerprints of Wright are as near as his emblematic central core chimney of Roman brick.

Left: The interior of the Brown House is rich with warm wood and wood tones, an important feature of a Wright house. The central hearth is executed in long, narrow, hard-pressed Roman brick, a modern touch of ancient artistry.

Above left: The interior of the Brown House contains built-in cabinetry designed by Wright, featuring handsome fine woods and art glass with nickel caming.

Above right: The horizontal character of Wright's Prairie form is continued on the interior of the Brown House with the use of high moldings and wood framing in the ceiling. Built-in furniture reflects his Prairie-centered artistry.

ROOKERY BUILDING: REMODELING OF ENTRYWAY AND LOBBY

Address: 209 S. LaSalle Street, Chicago, Illinois
Built: 1905

Daniel Burnham's Rookery (1886) is more than a Chicago landmark; it is a living piece of urban history, a sacred space emblematic of the city itself. Burnham, a partner in the firm of Burnham and Root, was the king of Chicago architecture. His crown was secured by the string of buildings of magnitude that made Chicago the envy of the nation. In addition, he was the architect of the World's Columbian Exposition of 1893, a showcase of inventiveness that brought twenty-six milllion visitors to Chicago and is said to have set architecture back fifty years because of its reliance on the historical neoclassical styles.

Wright was a young architect's assistant in the firm of Adler and Sullivan at the time and worked with Sullivan on his Transportation Building, a bright star of the event fashioned in the evocative Prairie style. Wright was always articulate about the failure to use an American style for the design of the fair. Burnham was a devoted friend of Wright's great patron Edward C. Waller. Waller's company managed the Rookery, so called because of a previous structure on the site in which birds nested in large abundance. Wright had his offices in the building in 1898 and 1899, as did

Left: The Rookery Building on LaSalle Street in Chicago, by Burnham and Root, is among the city's earliest and most treasured skyscrapers. The selection of Wright as the architect to remodel its grand interior was a mark of high distinction.

189

Above: Among Wright's most effective elements used in his remodeling of the Rookery Building was his use of lighting fixtures and lamps that added practical interior illumination and graceful, modern aesthetics.

Left: The interior of architects Daniel Burnham and John Wellborn Root's famed 1886 skyscraper, the Rookery Building, was remodeled by Wright, who added his Prairie style to the lobby.

Wright's River Forest client William Winslow and the American Luxfer Prism Company, the glass manufacturers whose work is used in such abundance in Wright's buildings. He also produced many designs for them.

So it is not surprising that Wright received the commission to redesign the lobby entranceway in what was then Chicago's grandest commercial building. Among the most significant Wrightian design elements to be introduced into the Rookery lobby was the white marble with exotic Persian-style ornamentation. It added a dramatic luxuriousness to the contours of the steel-sculptured interior, thick with Burnham and Roots's skeletal metal ribbing. The space is bright, open, and fresh, with a double curving set of stairways winding into the building's interior, heavy with metal ornament. The upper level of the lobby has a wraparound balcony that furthers the feeling of being in the interior of a clockwork. Wright's remodeling of the entrance opened it to a more expansive amount of available light. The interior is rich with elements of Prairie style, some of it the result of later renovation, conducted always with a unique reverence. In 1931, William Drummond, once an assistant in Wright's studio, introduced a further remodeling. The entire building received a massive restoration in the late 1980s that brought it back to life in a way it had not enjoyed in decades. It remains one of Chicago's most romantic and respected buildings. On LaSalle Street, the city's financial boulevard, it has heavy competition from neighbors such as the Chicago Board of Trade. The Rookery's pedigree as a Chicago building of prominence is only strengthened by its additional touch of Wright, making it his only contribution to the downtown cityscape.

Right: **Wright's remodeling of the Rookery Building, managed by his friend and client Edward C. Waller, introduced his dramatic Prairie style and added a deep sense of modernity in the simple but effective lighting design.**

E-Z POLISH FACTORY

Address: 3005–3017 West Carroll Street, Chicago, Illinois

Built: 1905

This rather simple commercial building on Chicago's West Side designed for the Martin brothers, William and Darwin, still stands. Though it is now windowless and a haunted shell of its brawny past, its sturdy design and modern functionality are still very much in evidence. It still enjoys a very central location, conveniently situated between Chicago's downtown and the suburb of Oak Park where William E. Martin lived in his three-story Prairie house designed by Wright. The Martin brothers were partners in this successful stove and shoe polish manufacturing enterprise in Chicago, the E-Z Polish Factory. Wright took up the commission to design and build this commercial structure while he was engaged in completing a commercial office structure for the Larkin Company of Buffalo, New York, of which Darwin Martin was the company secretary. Through his friendship with Darwin Martin, Wright received several commissions from Larkin executives for homes in the Buffalo area. Wright had befriended both Martin brothers when they paid a call on him at his studio while they were out motoring near his home. Their friendship grew as he finished the William Martin home in Oak Park and the Darwin Martin home in Buffalo.

While William Martin and Wright maintained a harmonious relationship during the construction phase of his home, the E-Z Polish project strained William's connection with Wright to the breaking point. William Martin became irate over Wright's inability to provide him with suitable design plans for the E-Z Polish Factory, even at the point when bulldozers began to remove earth for the foundation. All entreaties on Martin's part were thwarted by Wright, whose demeanor was exacerbated by rising financial costs and the architect's arrogant style. Even before the E-Z Polish Factory began to take shape, William had despaired of Wright's attitude, going so far as to question his sanity. "If he is sane," he wrote his brother, "he is dangerous."

Despite the strained air surrounding the development of this factory warehouse, the finished product can be said to have reached new levels of utilitarian artistry. There is nothing mundane about this industrial design. Originally designed as a two-story, the half-block-long structure is a dramatic expression of brick massing. Large horizontal rectangular windows were a familiar Wright staple here and help to establish the horizontal character of the building. At the same time, he used slender, brick pilasters projecting out from the exterior wall surface and running across the length of the façade to establish a sweeping verticality that was fresh and modern, certainly in 1905. The pilasters are graceful and, of course, deceptively utilitarian in their support of the outer wall design.

Right: The E-Z Polish Factory on Chicago's West Side is still an architectural wonder of good design and fine architectural artistry. The powerful brick pilasters provide a strong sense of vertical rise, while the wide, rectangular windows establish a strong horizontal expression.

They rise up from the ground level to just below the roofline, thus creating the effect of an industrial colonnade. The brickwork between floors runs in a horizontal line across the façade, expressing a strong sense of movement in the great brick mass. Following a fire in 1913, the building was enlarged with the addition of the upper three stories, which included the large "E-Z Shine Polish" sign executed in capital letters. At one time, a large mural of a Prairie house was painted on the main floor of the office area. With the Martin brothers' passion and patronage for architecture of Wright's Prairie design, the mural may have been their homage to the spirit of simplicity and utility on which their business was founded and that lived in such designs. Perhaps it was an expression of the harmony they sought, and often found, ravaged by Wright's antagonism.

Right: Due to a fire in 1913, the upper floors were rebuilt and many of the windows have been bricked in.

1906

PETER A. BEACHY HOUSE

Address: 238 Forest Avenue, Oak Park, Illinois
Built: 1906

The extensive piece of property on which this house sits is by far one of its most essential luxuries. It might well be the grandest of all Wright's Oak Park settings. An abiding sense of spaciousness is the overwhelming attribute at first glance, particularly when viewed from the side. The house is placed lengthwise on the lot. Though this house is proportioned on an extravagant scale, it is essentially a remodeling commission carried out while Wright was making his first journey to Japan, accompanied by his wife and Mr. and Mrs. Ward Willits of Highland Park, Illinois, for whom Wright had designed one of the first mature Prairie residences.

The significance of the timing of this trip is important in that it necessitated the hand and vigilance of a trusted architect from the Wright studio to carry the burden of the task. It is believed that Walter Burley Griffin was given this responsibility. His crisp hand was firmly holding the execution of this outstanding family residence for Peter A. Beachy, a successful banker.

Left: The Beachy House sits turned ninety degrees from the street. The flared roof has a unique gracefulness and pagodalike profile.

It is fitting that this elaborate house is located on Forest Avenue, a street encrusted with Wright houses of the highest quality.

Little of the previous house, said to be a small Gothic Victorian residence, remained through the remodeling—only some of the foundation. Taking full advantage of the proportions of the property, the new house is set at the very edge of the north line of the lot, similar to the position of the W. E. Martin House. The deep-set, gabled roof is distinguished by its central front peak and the wide eaves that flare flat out at the edge of the roofline, giving a touch of pagoda panache. Expanding across the length of the house on each side are three more scaled, repeating peaks that extend out over a series of three sets of cantilevered windows on the second floor. Their shape echoes the long roof that extends from the south end of the ground floor and expands the symmetry of the overall structure. Rose-toned common brick capped in limestone banding is used and rises up at the front to below the sill line at the front side of the house, while the brickwork reaches to below the eaves on the second floor. Brickwork capped with limestone also extends up to the sill line of the first floor and frames the exterior with a projected wall line with a horizontal sight line similar to that used at the Willits House.

Windowpanes throughout the house are framed in an intricate Prairie style, but without the embellishment of art glass. They ring the house in bands of glass that permit natural light to enter the house—a prerequisite of Mr. Beachy's. A man of invention, like other Wright clients, he also incorporated plans for a private laboratory to be located in a portion of the garage that also included living quarters for his driver. The interior of the house is very textured, rich with fine woods. Minimal work was done on the house until a 1990 fire caused damage to the front portion of the roof. This is a house on an unusually large scale in Prairie design.

Above: An aerial view of the Beachy House clearly shows its layout. It is constructed of brick and plaster with a wood trim; an earlier house constitutes part of the structure.

A. W. GRIDLEY HOUSE

Address: 637 N. Batavia Avenue, Batavia, Illinois
Built: 1906

Below: The expansive elegance of the Gridley House ranks it among one of Wright's most brilliant Prairie houses. A full-size Prairie dwelling, it is dramatically well proportioned.

The designs for the Gridley House have their origins in what might be Wright's most dramatic and rich periods of synthesis. Some of his most cherished and beautiful full Prairie dwellings were born in this creative year, 1906. In the town of Batavia, some thirty miles west of Chicago, Wright fashioned one of his most refined Prairie houses. Batavia is located in Kane County, a rural portion of the Illinois prairie in the early days of the twentieth century when Wright grew to know it. It was far west of Oak Park, along the rolling landscape of the Fox River Valley.

Gridley is said to have come to know Wright through his friendship with P. D. Hoyt, for whom Wright also designed a house in 1906 in the neighboring Fox River town of Geneva. Wright himself is said to have named this wonder of nature "Ravine Place" because of the rolling ravine of wildflowers that frame the southern exposure of the property. The house sits on more than two acres of land that is cradled by forest and prairie botanicals. Like other Wright homes, the Gridley House is dramatically organic, rising out of the heart of nature. The architect was often inspired by such locations of hearty geography.

This is a large fourteen-room, 5,000-square-foot structure that employs the familiar Wright cruciform plan along the lower level of the design. On the second story, the plans were altered to a T-plan. The five bedrooms, three full baths, and two half baths demonstrate the generous proportions of this stately Prairie dwelling. Three elegant, narrow, Roman-brick fireplaces are the center of interior family living, once again in rooms of generous proportions—a twenty-three by twenty-three-foot living room, a fourteen by twenty-three-foot dining room, a twenty-four by fifteen-foot kitchen, a fifteen by seventeen-foot den, an eleven by sixteen-foot maid's room, and an eleven by sixteen-foot open porch.

The spacious dimensions are reminiscent of the Willits House in Highland Park, with which the Gridley House shares other features. Most similar is the placement of the living room in one wing and the dining room in the other, enlarged by the connection to the porch. The exterior is fashioned of stucco and Cypress. Generous, graceful, hipped roofs slope in familiar sheltering eaves whose proportions provide the structure with its horizontal character. Also adding to that feature are the multipane sets of windows that deepen the Prairie style by their geometric order and precision. This is a house built for river-valley winds and prairie breezes that in the summer brought important refreshing air over the ridge along Batavia Road.

Right: Expansive cantilevering creates handsomely projecting hip roofs with powerful horizontal lines that extend in generous, sweeping size and proportion.

EDWARD R. HILLS HOUSE

Address: 313 Forest Avenue, Oak Park, Illinois
Built: 1906

This house fashioned for Mr. and Mrs. Edward R. Hills required Wright to completely redesign a house that had already been standing for more than twenty years. But it was not a commission Wright could refuse, as Mrs. Hills

was the daughter of a client, Nathan Moore, for whom he had designed the extravagant Tudor house on the neighboring lot. This house was to be a wedding present from Moore. When the project was completed, the Hills would reside next door to Moore, across a mini demesne of a backyard lawn, along a sizable stretch of Forest Avenue, by then an Oak Park architectural showplace. Across the street, the Hills could look out at the horizontal masterpiece of the Arthur Heurtley House. But in order for that to happen, Wright needed to turn the house some ninety degrees.

Among the most interesting features of the house is Wright's use of the flared, double-sloped roofs, which create a sweeping effect not unlike the Beachy House. Here, the pagoda patina he established has an even more decidedly Asian motif. The pointed, cantilevered hipped roof extending over the entryway is echoed in the high peak of the upper roof, best seen from the side view. Together they intensify that Asian thematic. While using his preferred exterior stucco-cladding, Wright deepens the sense of modernity with the crisp flatness it permits.

Banding below sill lines along the first and second floors presents a deeper sense of the horizontal to the exterior. This is further extended by the depth of the eaves on the second floor and the projecting roof above the third-floor, front-dormer window. The thick-framed windows are patterned with a nickel caming in the glass panes that are fashioned in a rectangular Prairie design. Set across the façade, they repeat the cantilevering in the windows also at the Beachy House. Wright returned to a style of sweeping roof treatment that he had not used in recent Prairie house designs. He achieved great verticality with the added height of the roof.

The best view of this house is from the north along Forest Avenue near the Moore House, which permits the true drama of the house to be seen. Mary and Edward Hills remained in the house until the early 1950s. A terrible fire damaged the house in the mid-1970s with the result that the second floor was completely destroyed. The house was rebuilt using the original plans. The backyard of the Hills House contained another architectural feature of note with the addition of one of Daniel Burnham's ticket booths left over from the World's Columbian Exposition of 1893. It is ironic that both the Hills House and the neighboring house of her father, Nathan Moore, were both nearly consumed by tragic fires, though some fifty years apart. Their survival is remarkable and their renovation and restoration to Wright's exacting specifications remain a testament to the resiliency and quality of his design.

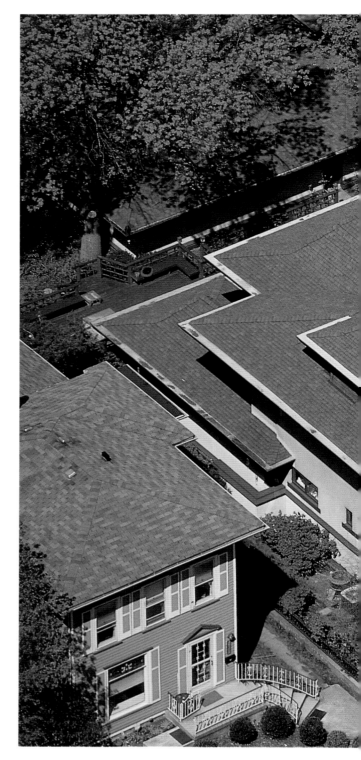

Previous page: Cantilevered roof projections add a curious elegance to this Prairie house that expresses Wright's sensitivity to the clean lines and utility of Asian artistry.

Above: Aerial view of the Hills House shows the expansive detailing of Wright's dramatic roof design and cantilevered projections.

A side view of the Hills House, looking south, highlights the deep symmetry of the entryway roof, whose horizontal proportion is balanced with the linear line at the rear of the structure.

P. D. HOYT HOUSE

Address: 318 South Fifth Street,
Geneva, Illinois
Built: 1906

Geneva has always been a remarkably quaint and picturesque town along the banks of the Fox River, a land that once was the home of the Potowatomie. Geneva is forty miles west of Chicago in rural Kane County, the same county in which Wright would build his Muirhead Farmhouse almost half a century later. Geneva had its origins in the same 1830s period of settlement as Chicago, though it remained a sleepy town until modern times. Mills and agriculture were the primary industries that surrounded this picture-postcard waterfront village. This geography was made to order for a Wright dwelling.

P. D. Hoyt was a well-known Geneva pharmacist when he became Wright's client. It is believed that the link between Hoyt and the architect was Hoyt's son Harrie, then an undergraduate at the University of Chicago. It is thought that P. D. Hoyt is responsible for introducing Wright to A. W. Gridley, for whom Wright also designed a house in Batavia in 1906. The Hoyt House does not have the voluminous grandeur of the massing Wright executed for Gridley. Instead, the Hoyt House demonstrates the gentility and grace of a comfortable English country cottage. It is imbued with a deeply organic quality that was always close to the heart of the architect. Designed in the square-plan mode, it is an earlier relative of the Hunt House and the Stockman House, though with enough variances to make the Hoyt House unique.

Here the architect fashioned a house with the odd feature of direct entry to the family living room. Unlike other square-plan types with side entranceways, the Hoyt House has its entry directly at the front with passage through a dramatic pergola, designed to surround everyone in nature. Generous room is made for the ample inclusion of flower boxes and the overhead trellis increasing the organic quality of the house from the very beginning. The pergola was removed in a later period, only to be restored recently. A similar

Left: A generously projecting trellis work, or pergola, canopies the entranceway to the Hoyt House, a dwelling entwined with the nature that surrounds it.

pergola passage on an even grander scale can be seen in the Wallis House in Lake Delavan, Wisconsin. The exterior of the Hoyt House is familiar stucco with stained wood trim. The hipped roof adds a gracefulness in its gentle sloping and a dramatic sense of protective sheltering from its overextending eaves. Each window carries a unique "H" monogram in the upper quarter of the panes, an unusual device rarely permitted in Wright dwellings. The Hoyt House demonstrates a civility that is richly scaled to human proportion and well suited for the quiet simplicity of this riverfront village.

Right: Wright created a generous country cottage in this Prairie-style house, rich in almost Elizabethan comfort, having deep overhangs, crisp stucco cladding with wood trim that fashions an important sight line, and an impressive pergola entrance.

Above: A powerful sense of modernity exudes from this stately Prairie residence built for George Madison Millard, extravagant with Wright's most significant elements of the Prairie style—gentle, hipped roof, deeply projecting, overhanging eaves, strong horizontal sight lines, horizontal board-and-batten, rough-hewed cladding, and an angle that gives the interior the most natural sunlight.

GEORGE MADISON MILLARD HOUSE

Address: 1689 Lake Avenue,
Highland Park, Illinois
Built: 1906

George Madison Millard was a noted Chicago bibliophile. His reverence for books, particularly rare books, moved him and fourteen other notable Chicagoans, including another Wright client, Chauncey Williams, to found the Caxton Club, one of the premier rare-book societies in the United States, in 1895. Millard spent his life in the pursuit of antiquarian books, with more than forty years as the celebrated owner of the A. C. McClurg Bookstore on Chicago's Wabash Avenue. Among the more outstanding features of the bookstore was its famous "Saints and Sinners Corner," originated by Millard, which soon became a gathering place for Chicago's most outspoken writers and free-thinking newspaper reporters.

But in addition to a passion for antiques, George Madison Millard and his wife, Alice Parsons Millard, twenty-nine years his junior, had their eyes fully fixed on the modern. Mrs. Millard was herself artistic, Wright recalled in later life. The Highland Park house that Wright designed for the Millards was a dramatic Prairie residence of cool angularity and expressive, cantilevered, hipped-roof artistry. The gentle rising of the roof is extended at the low-sloping eaves that project in deep overhangs. The flat edges of the rooflines create their own stylish statement, giving a more finished appearance. The exterior cladding of familiar board-and-batten planks enlivens the horizontal profile of the house and complements the rough-sawn movement that wraps the structure. The master bedroom on the second floor is cantilevered and extends over the long-profiled side porch.

The entire house sits sideways into the property, like many of Wright's other residences. Such a placement provides the house with a more practical use of the available land, as well as a more environmentally advantaged format. This is a house bathed in natural light, much of it available in the morning. For Wright, the harmonious setting of the house was as significant as its design elements. Windows here are plentiful and well proportioned for maximum light. They are nickel camed in a horizontal diamond shape. There is an open flow to the rooms on the first floor, from the living room through the dining room. The three bedrooms and two baths on the second floor are expansive by Wright standards, with the master bedroom having both a hearth and an outdoor balcony. The house has a full basement, unusual in a Wright house, that can accommodate a small living area for a staff member, in addition to the one on the first floor for a maid. This was Wright's first Millard commission. The Millards later moved to Pasadena, California, where, in 1923, Wright designed a house for Alice Millard after she was widowed. That house, known as "La Miniatura," was later referred to by Wright as his first Usonian house.

FREDERICK D. NICHOLS HOUSE

Address: 1136 Brassie Avenue,
Flossmoor, Illinois
Built: 1906

Flossmoor is a tony southern Chicago suburb of gentrified dwellings and picturesque avenues. The name's Scottish etymology means "gently rolling countryside." Flossmoor hit a boom in 1903 when the Illinois Central Railroad made it a stop on its commuter line to Chicago. Its life as a cozy Chicago bedroom suburb was set just three years before Wright designed the Nichols residence. Some confusion is still experienced over the correct name of this house, thanks to Wright's penchant for confusing and misspelling client names. Frederick Doveton Nichols Sr. is the client who commissioned Wright to build this golf hideaway that had neither electricity nor heat when it was first built.

The name Frederick Doveton Nichols has modern notoriety thanks to the distinguished career of the architect of the same name—the former chair of the Department of Architecture at the University of Virginia, Frederick Doveton Nichols Sr., and his son, the American artist Frederick Doveton Nichols Jr. While neither of them could have commissioned the house, it may be that a cousin also bearing the name was Wright's client.

Nichols was also involved in helping to finance Wright's 1908 Como Orchard Summer Colony and Bitterroot Project in Darby, Montana. Nichols met Wright through the Chicago financier W. I. Moody. The Nichols House in Flossmoor was essentially a summer getaway where Nichols could enjoy an uninterrupted game of golf. The house was clad in horizontal board-and-batten planks and was very much a version of the *Ladies' Home Journal* "Fireproof House for $5,000," similar to the Hunt House in LaGrange. Its simplicity and utilitarian design was suitable for Nichols's purpose.

Essentially this is a square-plan house with the first floor composed of a living room with a hearth taking up half the space, while the kitchen and dining room share the remaining area. The house was originally fashioned of redwood siding but was replaced with stained pine in the 1930s. Other renovations have altered the original façade to appear less rustic and more domestic. In fact, today the house has more than a small genetic relationship to the Johnson House on Lake Delavan, whose dramatic board-and-batten siding and sweeping hipped-roof overhangs appear similar. Of course the house today is but a shadow of its more primitive features that endeared it to Nichols. For more than half a century, the house was home to Melvin and Genevieve Evans, who refashioned the structure to fit the necessities of their family life. It is a house that has demonstrated a handsome modernity for almost a century.

Above: Wright achieves both vertical symmetry and horizontal proportion in the Nichols House, a dwelling rich in spacious, overhanging roof extensions and handsome rough-hewn pine boards.

Right: The low-sloping, hipped roofs of the Nichols House and the board-and-batten siding are reminiscent of the Jones House at Lake Delavan. Wright achieved a delicate symmetry in each house that sustained his Prairie aesthetic with simplicity and proportion.

The entrance to the River Forest Tennis Club is anchored by Wright's massive brick chimney block that carries the club logo, as well as the architect's Prairie aesthetic.

RIVER FOREST TENNIS CLUB

Address: 615 Lathrop Avenue, River Forest, Illinois
Built: 1906

This club in the exclusive Chicago suburb of River Forest is as well known for good tennis as it is for the architectural provenance of its Frank Lloyd Wright–designed clubhouse. The building was the product of Wright's studio, a collaboration of Wright and studio assistants Charles E. White and Vernon S. Watson. All three young men were members of the River Forest Tennis Club. Wright was thirty-nine years old when he designed the original structure, which was located at Harlem Avenue and Quick Street, along the eastern border of River Forest and Oak Park.

It was a replacement for the club's previous building, less than a year old, that was destroyed in a 1906 blaze. Wright's replacement was constructed in less than thirty days, making it, perhaps, his most swiftly fabricated structure. With a total cost of under $3,000, it might just be his least expensive structure. The building is surprisingly earmarked with many familiar Wright elements of design, like the long, low, hipped roof that was so much a part of Wright's Prairie style. Wright's use of horizontal board-and-batten cladding on the exterior wall surface is another standard element of his Prairie design motif, such as he used on the Davenport House in Oak Park. The long, low profile of the structure is emblematic of the Usonian design Wright employed many years later. Wright's task for the River Forest Tennis Club was to design a structure that would have high functionality and utility. His design was well suited for the high-level use of club members.

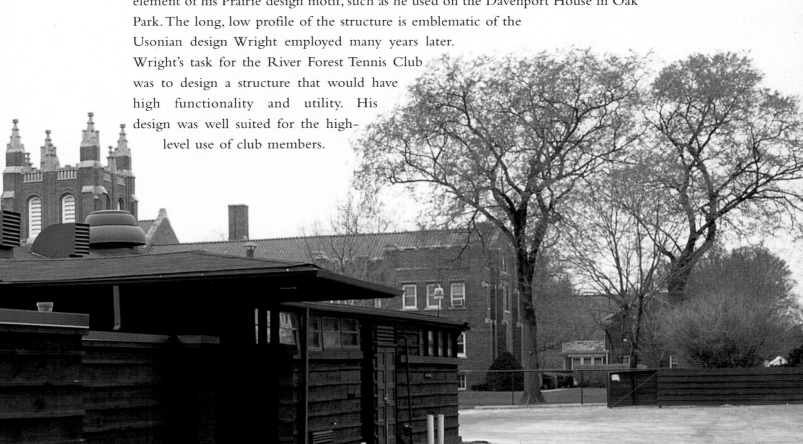

Double-paned, horizontal windows were set high in the low walls, permitting a large infusion of light while still maintaining a sufficient sense of privacy.

Perhaps most dramatically symbolic of Wright's Prairie style is the large, limestone-capped, Roman-brick chimney massing that carries Wright's geometric monogram in stylized letters. The verticality of this handsome brickwork is made even more dramatic by its unusual horizontal line created by its great width. It adds a simple but expansive rectangular geometry to the masonry plane, which dwarfs the overall club building. Wright designed three interior hearths, one on each wall, within the club's great central hall that accounts for more than half of the structure's design-plan space.

Expansive views of the tennis courts were made possible by the virtual wall of glass Wright created with the effective inclusion of fourteen glass-paneled doors that faced out to the courts. Expansive cantilevering was used in the roof design, as well as deep, sloping eaves, furthering the club's Prairie-style profile. The club sold its property to the Cook County Forest Preserve in 1920 and relocated to land further west in the suburb. The clubhouse was cut into three sections for the move and reassembled at its present Lathrop Avenue location. Vernon Watson oversaw an expansion of the club's facilities. Further buildings were added in the late 1980s by the fine Wrightian architect John Tilton. Over the years, he has carried out important restorations and additions to many Wright homes. His work has restored the essential character of Wright's original designs to the River Forest Tennis Club.

Left: An aerial perspective of the River Forest Tennis Club displays Wright's low-rising structures with expansively projecting rooflines.

FREDERICK C. ROBIE HOUSE

Address: 5757 South
Woodlawn Avenue,
Chicago, Illinois
Built: 1906

No house ever designed by Wright ever assumed such universal Prairie style sovereignty as the Robie House. Every detail of Prairie artistry came to maturity in this superb family residence within the shadow of the University of Chicago. Here, Wright developed his most revolutionary architecture. The Robie House is as fresh today as it was in that Edwardian age. Frederick Robie Sr. was only thirty years old when he commissioned Wright to design what has become his most famous Prairie house. He was an executive of his father's Excelsior Supply Company, a Chicago manufacturing firm that produced bicycles and that later was acquired by the Schwinn Company, the first name in American bicycles.

Robie was newly married and younger than Wright when he engaged his architectural services. Robie had a mechanical perspective for efficiency and sought a house that was both aesthetically pleasing and practical. His mind was as modern as Wright's. He yearned to be free of the clutter and "conglomeration" to which architecture had become tied. He had a specific list of architectural demands that others found too edgy for the times. Not so Frank Lloyd Wright. Most critically, Robie longed for rooms without interruption and windows without curvature. He wanted all the daylight he could get to fill his house and the ability to look out from his house

Right: The main rooms of family life at the Robie House, perhaps Wright's most famous domestic dwelling, are lifted high, to the second level, giving added privacy and a less obstructed panorama from the interior. Its multiple plateaus of soaring cantilevered roofs are among its most impressive architectural features.

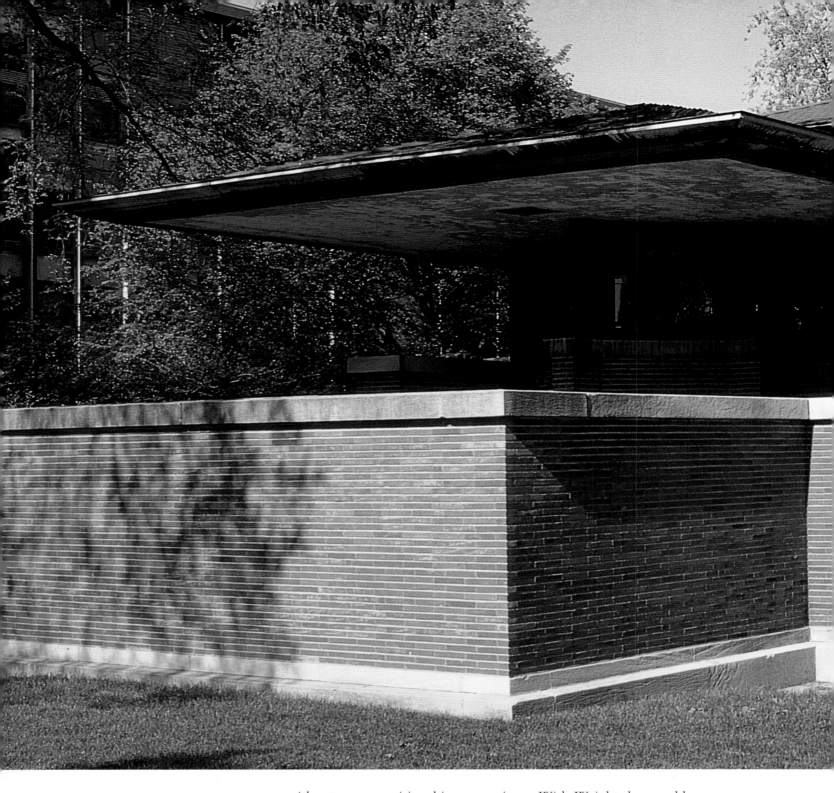

Above: Seen from an angle, the Robie House displays an extraordinary, extended cantilevered roof design that seems half a century ahead of its time.

without compromising his own privacy. With Wright, he would achieve all this and more to create a true classic of modern architecture.

The Robie House is an overwhelming visual sight, dramatic with the most expansive of horizontal proportions. Wright achieved this by his total use of narrow Roman brick that he had specially made in St. Louis. Each brick was one and a half inches thick and eleven and a half inches long. The backbone of the house was formed of fifteen-inch channel beams more than a hundred feet long, fabricated in Chicago by Ryerson Steel. This marked the first use of welded structural steel in an American house. In

addition to the sweeping cantilevering that is used throughout the structure, from the roofs to the family sofa, Wright exercised some dramatic experimentation within the project. Indirect lighting was used around the side walls of the living room. In addition, indirect heating, which Wright would use throughout his career with mixed results, was first introduced at the Robie House. Radiators were actually contained in the floors and heat rose from beneath the slabs. Robie relished the prospect of his feet never having to hit a cold floor.

When completed, Robie, to his delight, could look out of his front windows and see the Midway Plaisance, unobstructed, some two blocks away. In planning the construction of the Robie House, there was not a single cost overrun. Robie purchased the lot in Chicago's Hyde Park neighborhood for $14,000. The house itself

The interior of the Robie House is as dramatic as its exterior. Wright designed all the interior furnishings to create proportion and symmetry in every conceivable aspect of living.

Wright's Prairie style is reflected in this handsome wall sconce that re-creates the architectural cantilevering of the Robie House roof.

cost $35,000 to build, with Wright providing another $10,000 worth of built-in and Prairie-style furniture and interior embellishment. This brought the total to $59,000, which was $1,000 less than what Robie anticipated. Robie and Wright were mutually respectful of each other, while Robie gave Wright enormous credit for good planning. He always felt it "inconceivable that foresight, knowledge, and intense desire to do the right thing was imbedded in a man like him."

Not all the credit can be taken by Wright, for he took off for Japan as the project began, leaving it in the hands of an assistant named Mitchell to see it to completion. Robie noted that in conversation with the contractor, it was said that the plans were so perfect, he thought he

was building a piece of machinery. Fifty years later, in 1956, Frederick Robie Jr. met Wright in a Chicago hotel and introduced himself to the architect. Wright recalled with fondness the experience of designing his masterpiece of Prairie elegance with Robie's father. "A good house for a good man," was Wright's take on it. Today, the Robie House is owned by the University of Chicago, young Robie's alma mater and the place where his parents first met. Shortly before his death, Wright visited the house and declared it the finest home he ever designed.

Above: Wright's built-in furnishings are all complementary to each other and to the emphatic simplicity and utility of the Robie House interior.

Right: Wright filled the interior of the Robie House with a continuing expression of the Prairie style from the ceiling beams to the wood trim on the plaster walls, the art-glass windows, and the tall, spindle-back Prairie chairs.

1907

AVERY COONLEY HOUSE

Address: 281 Blooming Bank Road, Riverside, Illinois

Built: 1907

It is hard not to be overwhelmed by the sheer magnitude of the Coonley pavilions that frame this estate, as well as the drama that instantly engulfs anyone viewing this most extravagant of homes by Frank Lloyd Wright. Avery Coonley and his wife, Queene Ferry Coonley, were each the children of big Midwest fortunes—his, the Malleable Iron Company, and hers, the Ferry Seed Company. They were erudite and sophisticated, progressive and modern, and were products of elegant educations—Avery at Harvard and MIT and Queene at Vassar. Wealth, they understood, was used judiciously, not ostentatiously. Careful, thoughtful intelligence was the glue of their lives. Each was also a dedicated believer in Christian Science, with Queene an actual Christian Science practitioner.

Their Prairie palace, fashioned in the elegant Chicago suburb of Riverside, along the curving Des Plaines River, was set upon a natural peninsula that fit into the contours of that waterway. Frederick Law Olmsted, America's most substantive landscape architect, planned the design for this bucolic little town. As clients, the Coonleys were each younger than Wright and far more aristocratic than his usual type of self-made, quirky, commercial success stories. The refinements of their aesthetics were highly matured, especially in Queene Coonley, who had an expansive architectural knowledge, as well as a keen sense of appreciation for it. She was the driving force behind their selection of Wright for the commission of their new family home.

Left: A portion of the Coonley House garden, sculptured and formal, rich in botanicals that surround the Prairie character of this modern American palazzo.

Above: The Coonley House is classic Prairie style with the addition of exotic art glass bejeweled with turquoise and wrought-iron exterior railings. The horizontal sweep of the roofline is an essential element of Wright's style.

United in their aim to build a residence of high distinction, they went to Wright's Oak Park studio to offer him the commission because in his work, they told the architect, they saw "the countenance of principle." Wright always savored this as a great and honest compliment. As a result, he wrote, "I put the best in me in the Coonley House." What he gave them was a Prairie house, low, expansive, and imbued with many familiar Wright design elements, though fashioned in such a way as to be far more exotic and ebullient than anything he had ever done before. The Coonley House is acknowledged as Wright's first "zoned plan" residence. Here, the function and utility of a particular area of the house determines the rooms that will be placed there. The first zone, the ground floor, contains the entryway and the expanded play area for the Coonley children. Zone two is raised above the ground a full level, at the height of a regular second story, and

contains the public rooms—living room, dining room, kitchen, and staff facilities. A long connecting passageway leads to zone three, the bedroom area, which includes the master bedroom, children's bedrooms, and the guest accommodations. They are located away from the more public rooms for both privacy and quiet.

The roof is a low, hipped design that soars with broad, deep overhangs that provide the house with its dramatic character and clever technique for expanding shelter. The house appears to be a grouping of great pavilions, spatially linked through the sheltered loggias that are walled in glazed tiles in Cubist-design motifs. The exterior is clad in familiar Prairie stucco, embellished in places with more tiles. Three large, horizontally rectangular windows define the ground floor along the façade, while smaller vertically rectangular sets of windows define the second-level façade. The end pavilions have great, cantilevered roofs that flare, further intensifying the overall horizontal character of the house. A massive reflecting pool in front accentuates the lavish emotion of the house. Roman-brick hearths, rich woods, beamed ceilings, and art-glass skylights intensify the glittering Prairie character of the interior. The Coonleys moved to Washington, D.C., some eight years after the house was finished. In the 1950s, a pavilion of the main house and the additional structures built on the estate were sold and became separate residences. The house still thrives, filled with a unique light that Wright harnessed in this most dramatic of Prairie residences for the Coonleys, raising the profile of elegance forever in his Prairie design.

Left: **Wright embellished the exterior courts and walls of the Coonley House with glazed tiles in an exotic Persian geometric motif.**

Above: The upper portion of the Coonley House is enhanced with gigantic urns in a Prairie style.

Above top: A pergola fashioned in the Prairie style complements the natural environment around the Coonley House.

Above bottom: A portion of the Coonley House; Wright raised the living areas of the house to the second-floor level.

 COLONEL GEORGE
FABYAN HOUSE

Address: 1511 South Batavia Road,
Geneva, Illinois
Built: 1907

Though Colonel Fabyan might sound like a character out of an English mystery, he was very much a flesh-and-blood figure out in the Fox River Valley, west of Chicago in the early days of the twentieth century. The Boston-born Colonel Fabyan was the heir to a large textile fortune. While still in his late thirties, Fabyan and his wife, Nelle, purchased some ten acres of land in 1905, before seeing it grow to more than 350 acres in its heyday. Fabyan called his estate Riverbank, a property of remarkable curiosities containing everything from a zoo, windmill, Japanese garden, and lighthouse to a Roman swimming pool, boathouse, stone sculptures, and an old farmhouse.

It was the farmhouse that he commissioned Frank Lloyd Wright to redesign into a splendid country villa. Wright's efforts eventually engulfed the old structure. With the addition of a series of three verandas, the architect altered the basic plan of the structure from an L-shape to his preferred cruciform plan. A deep, peaked, gabled roof—reminiscent of the Jones House, Penwern, in Lake Delavan, Wisconsin—carries the crisp angularity and proportions of Wright's signature. A Prairie character revives the old farmhouse into a distinguished Arts and Crafts–style dwelling. Fabyan's passion for innovative utility matched Wright's own, with the result that the architect was encouraged to suspend interior furniture by cables from the rafters. The central veranda was built with an eastern view of the Fox River. A large, low-rising chimney sits in the roofline. Small paned windows, very similar to the Gridley windows, generously ribbon the house. Like many other Wright clients, Fabyan was a man of exceptional inventiveness and scientific learning. In 1912, his interests developed into Riverbank Laboratories, a center that specialized in the decoding and deciphering of enemy secrets.

In addition to such feats as using the works of William

Left: **Wright's renovation of the Fabyan House created a powerful sense of drama in the roof design and detail. He shaped a series of verandas that gave unfettered access to panoramic views of the nearby Fox River.**

Shakespeare to decode the Kaiser's secrets, Fabyan's laboratory conducted research in the areas of architectural acoustics, cryptography, and military weapons, as well as research into the use of tuning forks, the study of human anatomy, and human fitness. Riverbank also enjoyed enormous success during World War II and has been called the genesis of the Central Intelligence Agency. Alas, the colonel was not there to witness its success, having died in 1936 at the age of sixty-nine.

Above: Wright's dramatic roofline of the Fabyan House provides it with a sleek and graceful contour and complements the riverside environment.

Left: On the grounds of the Fabyan House, Wright further established his Prairie style with this shed.

STEPHEN M. B. HUNT HOUSE

Address: 345 Seventh Avenue, LaGrange, Illinois
Built: 1907

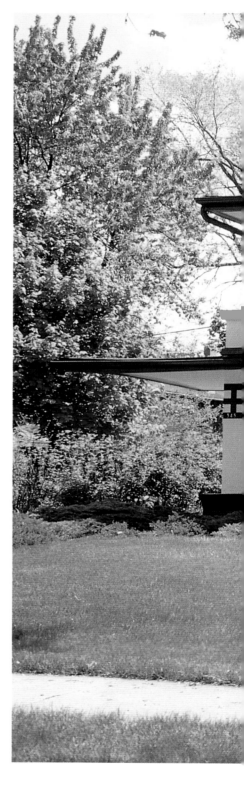

An evocative expression of the Prairie philosophy is articulated by Wright in his design for the Stephen M. B. Hunt House in the western Chicago suburb of LaGrange, an enclave of refined baronial residences that already boasted three early Wright dwellings, all bootlegged during his employment with Adler and Sullivan. This was his first home design to be built in that suburb in fourteen years, a critical period during which his Prairie style underwent dramatic evolution. Gone are the Victorian trappings of the Clark House's alpine roofs and the Queen Anne octagonal bays of the Emmond House. Wright's design for the Hunts is centered on a remarkable geometric cube, topped with a sleek, low-hung, hipped roof, expansive in its deeply sloping eaves that project an unmistakably uncluttered modern character.

The concept of this house was first portrayed in the April 1907 issue of *Ladies' Home Journal,* a national publication in which Wright unveiled his highly practical, modestly priced home for the American family—"A Fireproof House for $5,000." This was Wright's ultimate domestic residence for the average family. Wright was connecting the family of 1907 to their future, unfolding in the utilitarian aesthetics and rationality of a house for a new age, an era in which "safety" was an aggregate of wise, modern design. The architect achieved a dramatic sense of expansive proportion in the exterior massing of the stucco and wood cladding that defined the clean lines of the cube.

At the front of the house, on both the first and second floors, the horizontal lines of the house are enhanced by the window arrangement of one continuous, harmonious grouping of four panes of Cubist art glass, broadly framed. Those window lines are repeated around the second floor on each side of the house, permitting the remaining stucco façade on the ends to appear as wide, vertical pilasters sweeping from the ground to the roof line. Ground-floor roofs with deep, overhanging eaves project from both sides of the house. One extends over the entryway with a

Right: Bold vertical massing gives a dominant strength to the stucco exterior of the Hunt House. Powerful roof overhangs provide practical protective exterior sheltering and architectural elegance using the Prairie motif.

balcony above it. The other extends over a side porch that was later enclosed by the Hunts. Both extensions further enhance the horizontal sight lines. Wright incorporated a touch of Asian aesthetics in the caming of the windows and exterior ornamentation, extremely minimalist and geometric, not unlike the black modules that Dutch artist Piet Mondrian made famous.

The Hunt House is thought to be the very best of his "fireproof" design. The interior demonstrates Wright's passion for the continuous redefining of usable, practical space. This is a square-plan house in which Wright methodically arranged the floor plan according to its utility and function. This resulted in the living room taking up half the main floor, with an adjacent dining room opening off that, forming a large L-shape. Completing the plan is the kitchen. A large hearth of Tiffany brick is centered in the middle of this layout. Affordable housing was a significant theme throughout Wright's career, reaching a very tangible expression here in the Hunt House, built for $6,000. The floor plan is repeated later in Wright's American Systems-built houses, like the Hyde House. The Stockman House in Mason City, Iowa, totally replicates the design of the Hunt House. Wright would later design a second house for Stephen Hunt in Oshkosh, Wisconsin, an American Systems-built, single-story bungalow.

Left: The wide central chimney and graceful hipped roof are essential elements of Wright's unmistakable Prairie style in the Hunt House.

TOMEK HOUSE

Address: 150 Nuttall Road,
Riverside, Illinois
Built: 1907

One glimpse of the Tomek House is all it takes to discover the imaginative genius of Frank Lloyd Wright. Beyond all the other homes he designed, the Tomek House permits his real emotional character to be displayed. This is a house that soars, designed in an era when such technological accomplishments, seemingly magical, were rare. Emily and Fred Tomek, a real estate broker, engaged Wright to fashion this, their first real home. Wright's delight in the use of cantilevering makes this his most daring design. For many years, this critically important Wright residence was thought to have been designed later than it really was.

The Tomek House developed a nautical profile among locals, whose frame of reference was probably the great battleships of the day. The sweeping cantilevered roofs with their horizontal lines intrigued the public, shocked by the raw modernity that jumped up on the flat land of their prairie town. Riverside was the leafy enclave in which Joseph Lyman Silsbee, Wright's first architectural mentor and the man who first gave him a job in Chicago, built his own house along Nuttall Road. Wright was certainly designing and displaying a high level of artistry in creating this Prairie house wonder.

Wright sculpted the house in stucco, permitting him the opportunity to fashion exterior walls of flat, crisp, geometric verticality. The living quarters of the house are raised up a full level above the street, a design concept he employed also at the Thomas House in Oak Park and later at the Coonley House. In Prairie parlance, this living space was lifted off the plane of the prairie high above its earthy dampness and cold. It allowed the architect to lift the details of family life above the prying eyes of others, providing them with an added measure of privacy. This was a feature used with equal success at the Robie House. The main entrance is set low in the center of the façade on the ground level, sheltered by a cantilevered projection. Above, casement windows form a running ribbon of glass across the façade of the second level. The third level contains the house's three bedrooms in which Wright separates the

Right: The Tomek House has the lines and massing of a modern aircraft carrier—sleek, horizontal, and layered with decks. The entrance is set squarely at ground level within the sizable entry pilasters.

private area from the social area of the house by lifting it up high. The bedroom windows repeat the elegant zinc caming of the art glass in the geometric Prairie designs of the level below. Wright's windows add visual unity and horizontal harmony to the house.

At each end of the structure, wide, cantilevered roofs shelter the open porches. The east porch façade of the Tomek House and the south façade of Robie House share a very similar profile. Viewing the Tomek House from the west gives the most dynamic expression of the cantilevering and the massive pilasters mounted with expansive square Prairie urns. Their size creates a great visual illusion in their scale and proportions. When the urns are filled with plantings, nature is elevated to the level of the windows. The plateaus of the Tomek roofs receive structural lift and strength throughout from supports encased within the stucco pilasters. The central chimney flanks the upper level and contains the handsome hearths within the living area's interior. Beginning in the mid-1970s, a dramatic restoration was begun by Maya Moran, the artist/owner who lovingly returned the house to its original splendor. This was a heavy-duty structural renovation that strengthened important structural and aesthetic design components. Architect John Vinci served as a consultant for the project.

Right: An aerial view of the Tomek House from the front side shows the enormous flat roof with extensive cantilevered ends.

1908

ROBERT W. EVANS HOUSE

Address: 9914 South
Longwood Drive,
Chicago, Illinois
Built: 1908

Few houses designed by Wright have the dramatic landscape upon which the Evans House is perched. Situated in the richly forested and hilly terrain of the southern Chicago neighborhood of Beverly Hills, the house sits on the steep promontory known as the Blue Island Ridge, which naturally bisects this community. Longwood Drive is the stately, winding street that parallels the curving bottom of the ridge. The Evans House commands the top of a broad, rolling, grassy stretch of property rare in Chicago or any other urban neighborhood. It is land that Wright coveted for his expansive Prairie dwellings.

The house is a cherished part of the local landscape, baronial, aristocratic, and strangely similar to the Hunt House, though here the enlarged wings projecting on either side along the lower level expand the magnitude and horizontal profile of the house. The dark trim running along the rooflines and windows add an additional strength to the house's horizontal character. Because the elevation of the house is so powerful, the low-rising, hipped roofs and deep overhangs are even more dramatic than at the Hunt House. The profile, however, is unmistakable—the two-story, geometric cube with

Right: The Evans House sits high on a hill in Chicago's Beverly Hills neighborhood with a baronial Prairie splendor. Its dramatically large sloping lawn provides a setting that Wright cherished.

window-sets heavily framed, placed in the center of the façade. Here, however, Wright's stucco exterior cladding has been altered, replaced with a synthetic stone that stretches across the full front of the house. Both the south and north projections are also stone clad and have tall pillars topped with large urns. The sides and back sections of the house have exterior walls that retain the original stucco. The driveway along the north side of the house leads to a porte cochere off which an entryway and reception area are located.

Above: Detailed view of corner back area of the Evans House.

Left: The traditional stucco cladding of the Evans House façade was later covered in a stone veneer. Also visible are the extensive boards of banding that add so much horizontal character to the exterior of the house.

Wright designed the interior with an open living room that stretched the full width of the first floor. A dramatic, two-sided, Roman-brick fireplace separates the living room from the dining room. An abundance of bejeweled art glass encrusts the house and fills it with natural light. The dining room contains an extraordinary

art-glass light fixture that is set in the ceiling over the expanse of the table. It is one of the most striking remnants of Wright's careful original interior design. The house was historically filled with an abundance of magnificent custom furniture also designed by Wright that has been dispersed through the years by different owners. The Art Institute of Chicago houses much of the furniture and window glass, a library table, and a radiator cover in their collection.

The kitchen wing at the rear has undergone expansion and renovation through the years, but it still houses, unchanged, the white enamel and nickel built-in refrigerator that Wright installed almost one hundred years ago. The compressor is located in the basement and though its machinery requires constant attention, it still functions well. Elegant woods are used through the four-bedroom house whose low ceilings establish a warm, cozy environment throughout the interior. This is one of Wright's most spacious city homes, set in a historic terrain that provides the perfect marriage between architecture and geographical environment. So powerful was the introduction of Wright's revolutionary designs in the Beverly Hills neighborhood that soon smaller versions of the Prairie-style house were springing up, the work not of Wright, but of Walter Burley Griffin, his chief draftsman.

Above: This side perspective of the Evans House reveals its remarkably slender and soaring roofline and extensively projecting eaves, framed by tall pillars holding Wright's square, Prairie-style urns.

Right: The great jewel of the Evans House is the elegant art-glass ceiling light above the dining room table. Recessed into the ceiling, this large fixture is one of Wright's most important lasting decorative elements in any of his homes.

ISABEL ROBERTS HOUSE

Address: 603 Edgewood Place, River Forest, Illinois
Built: 1908

This house, like so much of Wright's personal life, is wrapped in a strange romanticism; much of it centered on Isabel Roberts, the young woman who served as Wright's office manager at the Oak Park Studio and the object of some considerable devotion on Wright's part. Isabel was the daughter of Charles E. Roberts, the automotive inventor and Wright's 1896 client who commissioned him to remodel his Daniel Burnham–designed Queen Anne house. Roberts went on to become a kind of patron of Wright, assisting in Wright's obtaining the commission for the Unity Temple, as well as other projects garnered from his assorted family members (the Bradley House and the Hickox House).

Half a century later, when Wright was remodeling the design for a new owner, he visited the house and showed affection for Isabel Roberts, encouraging the suggestion that during his betrayal of his wife, Catherine, with Mrs. Cheney, he may yet have betrayed them both with Miss Roberts. Wright also acknowledged to the new owners that some of the structural nightmares they were discovering were due to the fact that he was originally building the house as a "secret gift" for Miss Roberts and that he found it necessary to cut corners to save on expenses. That was little consolation to them as they uncovered further loose beams and unfastened supports.

What Wright designed, though, went beyond the realms of romance. He managed to create a house that was his most mature Prairie design in the cruciform plan. Its soaring cantilevered roof, for instance, has overhangs that seem to fly beyond the tall, two-story bay window of the living room, looking more like 1968 than 1908. The dining room and porch occupy the areas of the cross beams of the design plan that intersect in the living room. Wright placed the entry to the house in an almost hidden place in the corner at the juncture where the living room and dining room connect. Further touches of romance were carried out in the placement of a wrought-iron balcony outside Isabel Roberts's bedroom, replete with French doors. Two small iron seats were said to be placed on the balcony.

Originally the house was designed with a wood and stucco exterior, but in 1926 it was resurfaced in brick veneer. Wright filled the house with Prairie furniture to complement the daring character of the house. Though much of it survives, it is no longer in the house. Lattice-paned windows further add to the charm of the house that has remarkable horizontal lines defined by the flat roofs with powerful overhangs and further accentuated by the low walls that frame the front of the house. The presence of Wright's horse regularly tied up outside Miss Roberts's home on a Sunday morning seems to have been a source of some scandal in leafy River Forest. In the 1950s, Wright was in his eighties, yet he still perked up in warm reflection about the remarkable Miss Roberts, who ultimately never married.

Above: Wright produced an expansive, yet diminutive, cruciform, Prairie-style house for his studio's office manager, Isabel Roberts. It sits low to the ground with sweeping, horizontal, hipped roofs and a one-and-a-half-story central cube that is repeated in other Wright designs.

Inset: An aerial view of the Isabel Roberts House displays its cruciform plan, as well as the depth to which it sits on its narrow lot.

FRANK LLOYD WRIGHT'S LIFE 1900–1909

As the twentieth century dawned, Frank Lloyd Wright was galvanized by its power and its promise. Within its first ten years, he would engage in his most substantive designs, fashion the nation's most dramatic domestic dwellings, and reshape the contours of his personal life. He would design nearly a hundred buildings in which his signature style, reflecting the prowess and simplicity of the American prairie, engaged the landscape with a new intimacy. In the process, he would perfect the details and strategy of his organic architectural expression.

These early years of the new century also brought him into contact with a network of his most important clients—Edward C. Waller, William E. Martin, Frederick C. Robie, Colonel George Fabyan, and Avery Coonley. For them, Wright would design a singular concept of living: fresh, controversial, and uniquely American. Many would commission multiple structures from Wright for country cottages, warehouses, and large apartment complexes.

Wright's evolving Prairie-style homes always came with their own furniture, fixtures, and hardware—each piece incorporated by the will of the architect. His work was all about the entire complex of aesthetics. He provided more than merely the structure for a domestic dwelling, he reinterpreted for people how they should live and with what they should live. The suburbs around Chicago became thick during this period with the jarring spectacle of Wright's, at times, shocking aesthetic expressions. Dramatic overhangs, graceful rooflines, horizontal sight lines, and streamlined systems of cantilevered projections all demonstrated a new design style that was rich in its restrained refinements.

Wright was establishing Chicago and its nearby suburbs as the most architecturally progressive geography in America. His architecture fit the personalities and the achievements of his inventive, sophisticated clients. They had emerged from the Victorian age hungry for commercial and technological achievement. They saw in Wright the very symbol of the modern age that was coming into view. In his work, the embellishments and clutter that was so much a part of the previous generation was erased. In its place came a new certainty, a dramatic artistic simplicity, and a retempered understanding of the world, reflecting the fresh approaches in painting, music, and literature that were simultaneously emerging.

In addition to the substantive homes Wright had fashioned in Oak Park, River Forest, and the suburbs of Chicago's North Shore, he also designed five homes along the waters of Lake Delavan, Wisconsin, a community where many successful Chicagoans had country houses. He also designed country houses in Michigan, among which was a cottage on Marquette Island for Arthur

Right: **By 1909, Wright risked his professional reputation to abandon his wife and six children and run off to Europe with Mamah Borthwick Cheney, shown here in 1925.**

260

Heurtley, a client whose Oak Park house was a wonder of intricate, narrow Roman brick.

This was also a period in which Wright designed some of his most famous structures—the Ward Willits House in Highland Park (1901), the Larkin Company Administration Building (1903), the Unity Temple (1904), the Edward H. Cheney House (1903), the Frederick C. Robie House (1906), the Avery Coonley Villa and Estate (1907), and the J. Kibben Ingalls House (1909). His work was luxurious and sweepingly fresh, eliciting significant response from clients, critics, and the public.

Perhaps no house ever caused the controversy that the Edward H. Cheney House did. This two-story Oak Park bungalow, a jewel of architectural design, proved to be the undoing of Wright's local reputation when he began to carry on an affair with Mamah Borthwick Cheney, his client's wife and mother of their two children. By 1909, their love had moved Wright to risk his professional reputation, abandon his wife and six children and numerous architectural projects, and run off to Europe with the complicitous Mrs. Cheney. Design projects were left in the capable hands of studio assistants, including Marion Mahoney, John Von Bergen, and Herman Von Holst who oversaw completion. He made far fewer provisions for the protection of his wife and family. It was a scandal that would have destroyed lesser men. Without apology or contrition, Wright left Oak Park and set sail for Germany, bringing to a close his marriage, his reputation, and, for the present, his Oak Park career.

Right: Wright is shown in 1957 at the age of eighty-seven, pointing out features of the Robie House, which he called "the cornerstone of modern architecture."

1909

FRANK J. BAKER HOUSE

Address: 507 Lake Avenue,
Wilmette, Illinois
Built: 1909

The present owner of the Baker House is a retired architect who purchased the house in the early days of his marriage back in the 1950s. For him and his bride, it was love at first sight, for each other and for this remarkable house that was already almost fifty years old. Frank J. Baker, for whom Wright designed the expansive cruciform-plan house, was a public utility executive for the ubiquitous Samuel J. Insull when he built this modern, edgy Prairie residence in Wilmette, an elegant, North Shore Chicago suburb. Nothing like it had ever been seen there before. Baker, an attorney, would later become president of the First National Bank of Chicago. He helped to usher in a revolutionary new form of architecture in this enclave along the Lake Michigan shoreline.

There is a familiar echo in this design of Wright's of the Isabel Roberts House: the wide cantilevering of the central roof, the soaring verticality of the central windows in the main pavilion of the house, and the side projections of the cross-axis wings. Here, however, Wright has expanded the sheer length of the wings for Baker. The western wing along the entry drive, containing the day-to-day family entranceway, measures a full twenty-two feet and contains a reception room and dining room. The kitchen is located here as well. At the opposite end of the house, the east wing was originally a porch that is now enclosed. The main entrance is actually tucked into the front of the house not far from what is the most dramatic design feature, the two-story living room with cantilevered roof. The supports for the roof projection are actually

Left: The two-story living room of the Baker House has a dramatically wide, cantilevered roof. Six window mullions (central posts) provide added support.

the six mullions of the large, central, living-room window. This is a house of windows. They stretch from one end of the structure to the other, providing an unusual level of natural light.

The living room has the additional benefit of clerestory-style windows framing the upper level of the interior on two sides. The family sleeping quarters are located in an area at the rear of the house. This is an unusually wide house that sits on the property on an east-west axis facing north. Over the years, the planting of many Japanese pines that now tower over the house provide it with a mini forest to shield

it from Lake Street. The trees encircle the house and provide it with a kind of "Japanese-alpine" aristocracy. The exterior cladding is the original stucco and cypress that imbues the house with a sculptured grace, giving a hint, perhaps, of what the Isabel Roberts House may have looked like before the addition of its brick veneer.

The Baker House is a dwelling that has been well cared for. The present owner recalled a meeting with Wright not long after the purchase of the house. The young owners attended a conference sponsored by the American Institute of Architects at which Wright and Carl Sandburg were present. Shortly after entering, the couple spotted Wright and decided that they should approach him and inform him of their purchase of one of his homes. He was gracious, they recalled, and quickly asked which house they had bought. When informed that it was the Baker House, Wright said, "That's a great little house." The couple was chagrined, for they thought its five-bedroom spaciousness was bordering on baronial. Wright spoke about how much he liked the house and wished them well. As they walked away from the architect, he called after them. Raising his index finger and shaking it, he shouted a warning to them, "Don't wreck that house," he said half-humorously and probably half-seriously.

One look today and he would know they heeded his advice. This house is a treasure, lived in by people who knew how to negotiate a domain built by Wright. "The first thing we did," the present owner recalls, "was pull down all the heavy draperies that had been put up. They did not belong in a Wright house." The Baker House was built with the future in mind. Perhaps that is why it is possible to see in its simple, modern aesthetics the streamlined prefiguring of some of the revolutionary Usonian design structures Wright popularized in the 1950s.

Above: The sleek modernity of the Baker House is imbued with a simple design influenced by Japanese aesthetics.

Right: The Baker living room clerestory starts immediately from the floor-to-ceiling front windows.

WILLIAM H. COPELAND HOUSE

Address: 400 Forest Avenue,
Oak Park, Illinois
Built: 1909

Wright undertook a vast renovation of an Italianate residence for Dr. William H. Copeland, who had lived in the house since 1898. The rambling Victorian manse was originally built for William Harman in the early 1870s. It was the kind of splendid, baronial residence that shaped the

character of Oak Park in its pre-Wrightian period. In the late nineteenth century, small-town America was thick with such robust, two-story, classically tinged homes that demonstrated professional success and personal achievement.

The renovation of the house marked Wright's second commission from Copeland. In the previous year, Wright had been commissioned to design a stucco and wood–trimmed garage for Dr. Copeland in the Prairie style. Initial plans suggested that the house was to be refashioned as a three-story Prairie house, though that plan was rejected. Wright scaled back his redesign and developed a less severe direction for his work. On the exterior of the house, Wright's most substantive redesign was the roof that he completely replaced with a tile roof, though subsequent renovations removed it in the 1950s.

Below: **Wright's remodeling of this large 1873 Italianate house fused the character of the Prairie style to its exterior lines, none more powerful than the expansive new hipped roof, generous overhanging eaves, and a delightful wraparound porch.**

J. KIBBEN INGALLS HOUSE

Address: 562 Keystone Avenue, River Forest, Illinois

Built: 1909

This is a house dear to the heart of Frank Lloyd Wright. He relished visits to his friend Kibben Ingalls that always included Wright playing the piano. On one occasion, he was so taken with the visual beauty that encrusted the house, he told Ingalls that he had not charged him enough for so fine a house and entertained the idea that he might want more money. Ingalls would have none of this talk and told Wright he had been fairly paid and that if he persisted, he would have no alternative but to toss him out. Wright continued to play the piano. J. Kibben Ingalls was a successful Chicago railroad business executive, as president of both the Northwestern Refrigerator Line Company and the Western Refrigerator Line Company. He was just thirty-nine years old when he commissioned Wright to design this grand Prairie-style residence. The house was under construction when Wright left Oak Park with his lover, Mamah Cheney, for his extended European hiatus. The completion of the project was turned over to his assistant Herman Von Holst.

Designed in the form of a Greek cross, the Ingalls House is one of Wright's most mature Prairie designs. It has a dramatic sophistication and is fashioned in an almost regal opulence. Among the special wishes of the client was that every room in the house should have windows on three sides. The result was not just a significant infusion of natural lighting, but also an unusual cross ventilation that emerged out of the Ingalls family's sad profusion of childhood disease. Windows here are bejeweled art glass with copper caming. They are perhaps the most elegant of any Wright house. The house sits on a lot of unusual proportions, fifty feet wide and 270 feet deep. From the front, the house is dramatically defined by the expansive, cantilevered, low, hipped roof over the living room and veranda that is fitted with large screens for the summer. Its gently sloping eaves are repeated on the upper roof. The roofline also helps to establish the decidedly horizontal character of the house. The wide, low rise of the central chimney appears to fill the entire center

Right: Wright imbued the Ingalls House with an elegant symmetry and a splendid horizontal profile that has few rivals.

of the upper hipped roof. The edging of the roofs and chimney are wide, strengthening the horizontal planes, and are repeated in the capping of the veranda wall and the belt coursing under the sill line of the second story.

The present owner is a distinguished architect who previously lived in the Beachy House in Oak Park. He has been responsible for the renovation of a number of important Wright designs that include the Meyer May House, the Johnson Wax Building, the River Forest Tennis Club, the Wright Home and Studio, and the Hills House. He also designed an expansive rear extension for his own house that enlarged the footprint of the cruciform design. The rear profile now includes a substantial family room and redesigned open kitchen that flows to the expansive rear terrace. The interior is bright and richly textured, with handsome white oak, a favorite of Wright's. Side balconies are cantilevered off upper-level bedrooms. The house enjoys an unusual connection with the environment front and back. Set out further than many of the other houses on the block, the panorama from the front veranda enjoys a view to the north and south that is unbroken by any neighbor's home, only by the rolling, tree-rich lawns of stately Keystone Avenue.

Below left: Extensive cantilevered balconies add to the horizontal character of the Ingalls House, accentuated by the color scheme for the exterior banding.

Below right: The Ingalls House is currently owned by a prestigious architect who has worked on many restorations of Wright homes around the country, including the Meyer May House. He has enlarged the cruciform plan of his own house with this rear extension that contains the kitchen and family room.

Above: The Ingalls House boasts an extraordinarily expansive, cantilevered, low, hipped roof that essentially defines the house.

1911

OSCAR B. BALCH HOUSE

Address: 611 North Kenilworth Avenue, Oak Park, Illinois
Built: 1911

This stately residence was Wright's second commission from Oak Park interior designer Oscar Balch. Some five years earlier, some time after Wright's return from his first Japanese travels, the architect remodeled a Lake Street storefront for the design firm of Peebles and Balch. Long since demolished, the building displayed a remarkably fresh chic that showed the influence of the Orient in increasingly fashionable Oak Park. Once again, Balch became an important client for Wright following his return from travel; this time from his extended European adventure with Mamah Cheney. In the scandalous display of open disregard for public morality, Wright lost friends, clients, and his family. There were, however, a coterie of admirers who stood by him. Most critical were those who still looked to Wright for a dramatic architectural design that was as startling as his personal life. Oscar Balch was one such client. In addition to the curious provenance that this house endures as Wright's defiant gauntlet of return to the shady streets of Oak Park, the house is significant because it marks his return to architecture after a hiatus in which anything might have happened. It is a house forged of Wright's personal courage and cheeky moral humbridge. His grand design, however, evokes no such spite. Instead, Wright produced a house of refined civility, vastly geometric, stirringly horizontal, and expressive of an odd maturation despite his personal moral failings.

However, one does not need to be a psychiatrist to see, in the symbolic nature of the heightened terrace walls, the precaution of the security wall, or the obscured entryway to recognize the telltale signs of someone feeling "under siege." It was not Oscar Balch that was under attack. Perhaps it is a glimpse of Wright's subconscious: a rarity. But it in no way does it detract from the beauty and the remarkable linear proportion of the house. Wright brought a new architectural drama to Prairie design with his use of the flat roofs. Their tabletop expansiveness is a further refinement of Prairie simplicity. There is a familiar shadow here of his pavilion expanse that he used on such a grand scale at the Coonley House. Here, he raised the horizontal eye line with the ribbons of windows that run around the second story, their sturdy mullions reflecting the capping of the dormer tower, the roof edge, the chimney, the veranda, and the privacy wall. The capping device becomes a unifying design feature. The living room, with a handsome narrow, Roman-brick fireplace, anchors the house at its center. Small, set-

Right: **Flat, crisp, expansive rooflines, expressive exterior massing, and strong Prairie detailing, such as fifty casement windows, mark Wright's first efforts in Oak Park following his return from Europe. Privacy walls may be indicative of his personal sense of a state of siege.**

back side pavilions, with libraries on either side, expand the symmetry and flow across the expanse of the house. The volume of window glass brings a familiar interior lighting from nature. Broad, flat overhangs extend the Prairie shelter theme. Exterior stucco cladding provides the house with its finessed sculpturing. On the opposite side of Kenilworth Street from Balch, Ernest Hemingway spent his adolescence.

Above: The Coonley Gardener's Cottage sits deeply into the flat soil of the prairie with a profound horizontal character further sustained by the long, sleek, overhanging eaves.

AVERY COONLEY GARDENER'S COTTAGE

Address: 290 Scottswood Road, Riverside, Illinois
Built: 1911

Wright endured a complicated period in his personal and professional life following his return from Europe in 1911. Often he was galvanized by clients who cheered his return to design work. No one was more elated than Avery Coonley, the erudite aristocrat for whom Wright had previously designed a great Prairie estate. Coonley expanded the character of his demesne with the addition of several buildings to house his staff. Not one to scrimp on the aesthetics, Coonley had Wright fashion these smaller domestic dwellings. While they are dwarfed by the magnitude of the Coonley house, they are gems of architectural grace. The gardener's cottage is a perfect example. It is a testament to Coonley's remarkable Christian Science gallantry that he would create such suitable lodging for those on his payroll. It should also be noted that in Riverside, the bucolic paradise that Frederick Law Olmsted, America's foremost landscape architect, designed, and which years later landscape genius Jens Jensen reconstituted, the gardener was truly king. Here, he was not just someone to rake the leaves and trim the hedges. In Riverside, he was the overseer of nature's bounty and rarified horticultural patrimony. The handsome Prairie cottage designed by Wright reflected the eminence in which a tender of gardens was held.

In the 1950s, this building, along with other Coonley structures, was separated from the larger estate and sold to private owners. Today, the Coonley Gardener's Cottage continues to enjoy a rich celebrity. The present owners are professionally engaged in architectural gardening and design. Delighted at owning such a landmark, they maintain the grounds with true Prairie growths. The house is intimate with the nature that surrounds it, sitting low to the ground, with gently sloping, hipped roofs and deep-set overhangs. A broad brick chimney anchors the cozy, diminutive character of the house and defines the central axis of the interior hearth. Wright is reverenced here, along with some of his students whose work lines the wildly curving streets of this village still lit with gas lamps. To offset the tiny scale of the house, Wright embellished it everywhere with windows that let in both nature and light. The cottage carries the thematic exterior cladding of the main house. Its stucco and wood are a mark of its Prairie pedigree and its unbroken reflection of the big house. Proportion and scale are design devices here in what might be Wright's coziest Prairie nest.

Right: The massive central chimney of the Coonley Gardener's Cottage is a constant of Prairie architectural design and strengthens the cozy character of this dwelling.

AVERY COONLEY STABLES/COACH HOUSE

Address: 336 Scottswood Road, Riverside, Illinois

Built: 1911

It is a significant aspect of Wright's remarkable design for the Coonley Estate that when the grounds of the villa were split up and the structures separated and sold between 1952 and 1957, that a building created specifically for utilitarian purposes, first as a stable and then as a garage, should make the transition so easily and elegantly to a private family home. Despite the sad reality that the estate had to be broken up, it remains remarkable that the buildings still stand and remain in use. After all, they could easily have passed the way of the Edward C. Waller Estate, just miles north along the same Des Plaines River. Wright's original design for the Coonley Estate had long-lasting life for each of the structures. The stunning aesthetics and architectural beauty of the stables remain both a tribute to the architect and to the Coonleys, who were people of taste and vision. The creamy stucco and wood exterior of the stables is a gentle massing and, of course, relates in a more subdued manner to the overall design of the main Coonley Villa.

An unembellished horizontal line is enhanced by the plane of the gently sloping and projecting hipped roof and the double ribbon of cubed windows that deepen the long horizontal character of the stables. Large stucco planter boxes stand high as a botanical wall beneath the sill line of the structure's windows. The square character of the fenestration is reminiscent of the Tomek House, a Riverside neighbor. The stable/garage is located just behind the gardener's cottage and, much like it, seems to be arising out of nature, Wright's most enduring organic concept. The projection of the roof demonstrates a deep cantilevering that is an aesthetic tool of the overall estate. The stable chimney is large, wide, and demonstrably one of Wright's grandest. The extensive Cubist geometric patterning that Wright used with ample flourish here in the stables has a definite Japanese flavoring, more so than the exoticism of the main villa and the genteel simplicity of the gardener's cottage. There is a curious genetic tie to the house he later

Left: The Coonley Coach House is today an independent dwelling typical of the Prairie style. A massive chimney and geometric windows are signature elements of Wright's design.

designed in 1918 for Arinobu Fukuhara in Japan that perished in the great earthquake of 1923. The Coonley Stables is one of Wright's truly lovely homes, a dwelling with a second life that was not intended, but that flows as the result of great architectural design.

Left top: A side view of the Coonley Coach House shows Wright's square-window treatment and wide side box filled with plantings that lift an element of nature to the level of the windows.

Left bottom: Side view of the Coonley Coach House. Exterior banding and deep eaves enhance the horizontal character of this unique Wright dwelling.

Above: The rear of the Coonley Coach House demonstrates Wright's passion for crisp geometric shapes. The exterior of the house is enhanced by the addition of a wide planting box to the exterior wall.

1912

AVERY COONLEY PLAYHOUSE

Address: 350 Fairbanks Road, Riverside, Illinois
Built: 1912

There is a remarkable majesty to this most curious of Wright designs, the Coonley Playhouse. Today, it is, of course, a family home. But when it was conceived, it was an ongoing component of the grandeur of the Coonley estate. Though not contiguous to the original set of gated Coonley buildings, it is just a few twisting curves away in the forested terrain of Riverside, still abounding with the landscape designs of Olmstead and Jensen. The structure was designed as the ultimate luxury, a private schoolhouse for the Coonleys' daughter and the neighborhood children. Mrs. Coonley staged plays there with local students. Wright filled the structure with rich, playfully imaginative glass—confetti and balloons in bright primary colors—creating an environment for the amusement and education of children. Today, this glass can be seen at the Metropolitan Museum of Art in New York. This is an important structure, demonstrating Wright's ability to adapt and evolve. Though filled with obvious Prairie-style inclusions, there is a strong expression here of styles that would become widely used by him in California and Arizona in the future.

The playhouse was designed in the cruciform style and contained a stage and a large room for productions. An area in which to construct theatrical props and a kitchen were also included. The playhouse has long since been refashioned into a domestic residence. It easily makes the transition to a stately Wright home. A two-story pavilion soars high at the center, with smaller one-story pavilions on either side, set back. They reflect the second level of the Coonley House, but also recall the handsome tall, central pavilions at the Baker House and the Isabel Roberts House. Flat roofs project out over the façade. The center eave is open, permitting light to hit the façade and decorative windows. Twenty-two clerestory windows ribbon the interior of the living room. Though the originals are museum treasures, new high-tech decorative art glass has been installed, providing the expansive interior of the great room with dancing jeweled light. The front windows are tall and expansive, with three narrow, central windows running the full vertical sweep of the façade. The cantilevered central eave is supported by the four mullions of the central window. They stand like narrow columns, enhancing the verticality of the façade. Similar open-cantilevered eaves project from below the line of clerestory windows of the living room, further extending the natural light

Right: **The Coonley Playhouse has great vertical lift, forming a two-story cube in this central portion of what is now an independent dwelling. Powerful, cantilevered eaves projecting from the roofline have gaps to permit more natural light to fill the interior.**

on the structure during the day. Shade is minimized by them. The main entryway is at the right side of the house, along the driveway. Prairie architect William Drummond, who fashioned several homes in Riverside, designed the garage for the playhouse in 1919. The playhouse's interior views, always a significant Wright consideration, are lush, dominated by a vast panorama of oaks and sprawling public parkland that provide this whimsical Wright creation with visual splendor.

Above: The cantilevered projecting overhang from the Coonley Playhouse roof is open-worked to permit a maximum of natural light into the interior.

Right: Detail of a window at the Coonley Playhouse.

Right: Vertical beams are actually the window mullions of the central cube of the Coonley Playhouse that further support the deeply projected cantilevered eaves.

WILLIAM B. GREENE HOUSE

Address: 1300 Garfield Avenue,
Aurora, Illinois
Built: 1912

Wright's house for William B. Greene is a late Prairie design set in the city of Aurora, Illinois, a large municipality some forty miles due west of Chicago. Together with the houses designed for P. D. Hoyt, A. W. Gridley, and Colonel Fabyan, the Greene House sits within the shadow of the Fox River Valley. The Fox River was an important natural resource and commercial engine that helped to settle the region that remains Chicago's nearest rural neighbor. Greene himself is emblematic of many of Wright's early clients, individuals whose professional careers involved the emerging technological and electrical wonders of the twentieth century. A mechanical engineer with a degree from the University of Illinois, Greene was only twenty-six years old when he commissioned Wright to design his Prairie dwelling. His company, Barber-Greene, became the world's largest producer of machinery for asphalt paving. Youth and passionate inventiveness are probably the two elements of closest commonality among Wright's remarkable client list.

This is a large, spacious Wright design, very much an example of the Fireproof House that the architect popularized among his more savvy, economical-minded clients. The exterior cladding is traditional stucco with stained cypress-wood trim. A great horizontal simplicity demonstrates one of Wright's most well-perfected design features. The hipped roof is low, more flat than usual, with deep projecting eaves. Criticism abounds that Wright's studio draftsman, Harry Robinson, the college roommate of Greene, not only supervised the project, but made alterations to the designs. In the late 1920s, Robinson was brought back to direct an expansion of both the dining room and the master bedroom.

The open porch was enclosed by Greene's son during renovations in the early 1960s. The house also has some fine examples of the window design from the Wright studio that are unusually large and generous in a Wright Prairie house. Wright repeats his use

Right: The interior of the Greene House features Wright's essential central hearth, an element of design that links all his homes together. Windows are large to maximize natural light, with the lower portion of the windows taller than the upper portion to eliminate the obscuring of the view.

of a large pergola as a constituent part of the exterior design, as he did at the Hoyt House. It further helps to display the rich and ripe presence of nature as a physical expression of the overall design. While much of the Wright-designed interior furniture has been sold, the Greene House remains an important element of Aurora, "the City of Lights."

Right: Wright expands his Fireproof House plan in the late Prairie-style of the Greene House, a large dwelling with a stucco and stained-cypress exterior cladding.

1913

HARRY S. ADAMS HOUSE

Address: 710 Augusta Boulevard, Oak Park, Illinois
Built: 1913

The Harry S. Adams House is a rich and textured dwelling, encrusted with Wright's mature Prairie character. From roofline to bejeweled art glass, this is a design of singular expression and noteworthy details. It is perhaps Wright's saddest house, for it brings to an end his Oak Park career and his intimate connection to this lush, cozy Chicago suburb. As the last house Wright designed in Oak Park, it represents a great moment of change in the architect's life. This house is a synthesis and summation of his Prairie aesthetic. He was a man on the move personally and professionally. Personally, he left behind the community, clients, neighbors, and family that for many years were the inspiration for his family-centered Prairie houses so tied to the land and the values of the prairie. Taliesin in nearby Wisconsin was to be the center of the next phase of his life. Professionally, he had already begun to move away from the Prairie motif after his European break. At this time it was twenty-four years since he first designed his home and studio on Chicago Avenue. New ideas were on the horizon. But here, for a last moment, he brought together the refinement of his ideal.

The Adams House was built on a grand scale, stretching the width of almost three Chicago-size lots, seventy

Left: The façade of the Harry S. Adams House has an expansively wide horizontal sweep of seventy feet. The extensive projection of the bilevel eaves provides a broad sheltering.

295

feet from east to west. The expansive width of this property permitted Wright to unleash the full throttle of his horizontal form. Low-sloping, hipped roofs with deep, projecting overhangs accentuate the horizontal profile, aided by the limestone string banding that further defines the horizontal line at the top of the massively wide, central chimney, underneath the sill line on the second floor, and along the top of the low wall across the façade. Prairie urns, cubic and gracefully thin, define the entryway. Honey-toned Roman brick coats the house with a strong modernity. Ninety years later it is still fresh and elegant, providing aristocratic architectural elegance. Casement windows add rectangular

Above: This aerial view of the Adams House demonstrates the remarkable gently sloping, hipped roofs and the simplicity of its horizontal character. The low-rising front wall adds a perfectly balanced symmetry.

geometry, as does the limestone-framed, three-part window in the dining room on the right side of the façade. The roof of the porte cochere extends the low-rise Prairie design across the left side of the façade. Designed with four bedrooms and three baths, this was ultimate luxury in a Prairie house. Wright's most stirring design feature for the Adams House was saved for the front door. Exquisite art glass transformed the front door into a masterpiece of Prairie artistry, filling the interior entryway with dancing color and shimmering light, an appropriate touch for the last house made by Wright in a leafy village that was the making of him.

1915

EMIL BACH HOUSE

Address: 7415 North Sheridan Road, Chicago, Illinois

Built: 1915

The residence that Wright designed for Emil Bach, co-owner of the Bach Brick Company, is a music box of a house, square, compact, high, horizontal, and tuneful. Built on Sheridan Road, the city's great lakefront thoroughfare that is sometimes slapped with cold Lake Michigan winter water, this is a true city house. It stands in a neighborhood thick with expansive period manses, brick Chicago six-flats and high-rise condominiums with breathtaking views of the lake and downtown cityscape. This Rogers Park neighborhood is Chicago's northernmost outpost, bordering the city of Evanston just a few blocks north.

The Emil Bach House is all that is left of Wright's few North Side Chicago residences, the Husser House, Harlan House, Horner House, MacHarg House, and Steffens House having long ago been demolished. The Steffens Residence (1909) was a nearby neighbor to the Bach House, just two blocks north on Sheridan Road. Bach's house is also significant as Wright's last venture in designing a small, urban dwelling. There is no denying the tightly compacted form of this cruciform structure; on a site that is set within the constrictions of a location in the middle of a block. Taking this into account, Wright expands the architectural opportunities available to him for furthering privacy for his client. He located the main entry, for instance, at the side of the structure, away from busy Sheridan Road, virtually hidden from public view. The front door actually faces the rear of the house, accessed only by way of a paved walkway from the street and up a flight of stairs. The main doorway can only be reached through the patio. Small casement windows concealed beneath broad, projecting overhangs further enhance his design for privacy.

The footprint of the structure is that of a condensed rectangle measuring forty-one feet by fifty-two feet. This house is, as Wright always sought to do, one with its location. But here, it is not so much the flat land of the prairie or the shoreline of Lake Michigan that must be taken into account, but rather a crowded urban location where houses do not have the luxurious breadth and width of generously proportioned lots, like Oak Park and River Forest. Wright demonstrated an interesting urban sensitivity with the placement of this house. The roof is flat, with expansive, cantilevered projections that add a comforting sense of shelter. On the first floor, along Sheridan Road, the living room projects out from the exterior walls of the central core of the rectangle. So, too, does the first floor's rear porch. Windows across the first floor are deep-set, heavily framed by wide brick mullions that encase the fenestration. The brickwork is extensive. The

Right: The Bach House, Wright's last Chicago dwelling, is an intricate Prairie-style dwelling with wide, extending roof projections in the center of a busy urban block.

exterior walls are a mix, tawny brick across the first floor and cream-colored stucco and wood across the second. The second floor has cantilevered room projections at each arm of the cruciform. The multiplicity of such projections, across the whole structure, intensifies the Cubist aesthetic of the house.

On the interior, the first floor is anchored around the central fireplace and staircase. The interior trim replicates the horizontal projection of the exterior with strong geometric lines. Interior walls are finished in a light cream "pebble-and-sand plaster." Wright chose the interior color and named it "sunshine." All wood trim and built-in furniture is of black walnut, said to be cut from one tree. The architect went to great lengths to create an environment that sheltered the client from the urban reality outside the house. Wright was still reeling from the tragic murders of his lover, Mamah Cheney, and her children by a deranged servant at Taliesin. Keeping the world at bay was an architectural priority. With this intensely geometric house, Wright says good-bye to small dwellings. In the Emil Bach House, Wright destroys the box, the shape to which most architecture was constricted. For Wright, the inside and outside of the house are as one.

SHERMAN M. BOOTH COTTAGE

Address: 239 Franklin Street,
Glencoe, Illinois
Built: 1915

This is a house rich in romantic lore and polished with the sparkle of an uncomplicated dwelling set into the heart of nature. It is said that Sherman Booth, Wright's Chicago attorney, helped to untangle many of Wright's financial difficulties. He commissioned this one-story cottage as a wedding present for his wife, Elizabeth, giving the house its unusual pedigree as a "honeymoon cottage." The house was originally built on property owned by Sherman Booth and was later moved in 1915 to its present Franklin Street location in the North Shore lakefront community of Glencoe, some thirty-five miles from Chicago. Glencoe is also the site of Wright's Glasner House (1905). In the deeply forested geography of early twentieth-century Glencoe, this cozy, timbered cottage had a "magic garden" persona. It was honeymoon heaven for the Booths and for a later pair of newlyweds who made it their own honeymoon home in 1956.

The present owner, a now-retired architect, purchased the cottage just after his marriage. He and his bride have lived there ever since, making some needed expansions for their growing family over the years. For them, the house has always had strong connections to Wright, whom they met on a few occasions in the mid-1950s. In fact, the owner recalls, as a young boy in the 1930s, reading the *New York Times* with his father while staying at the Plaza Hotel on a visit to New York; the feature they read focused on the controversy surrounding Wright's construction of the Johnson Wax buildings in Racine, Wisconsin, and on the viability of the proposed radically new load-bearing columns. It filled the boy with interest and delight. "I think I wanted to be an architect after that experience," he said.

The cottage sits low to the ground, flat roofed, with an expansive porte cochere. A curved drive circles from one side of the property to the other around an expansive front lawn. The proportions of the lawn further define the scale of the house that is intimately related to the nature that surrounds it. A powerful horizontal line unfolds in the board-and-

Right: The Booth Cottage sits low to the ground, evocative of the Prairie style.

batten cladding that is modern and simple, not unlike the Usonian
style Wright was to develop throughout the 1940s and 1950s.
Rectangular windows add verticality to the house and an
uncomplicated grace with their ladder caming, making a handsome
Prairie motif. The darkly stained wood exterior is almost a natural
camouflage in its present setting. The low rise of the structure
makes it easy to envelope it in thoughtfully placed shrubs and
tasteful succulents.

The house today is more Wrightian than ever. The owner made a careful restoration of the floors, using oak in places where Wright first used fir. A large canvas cloth that once covered the ceiling in the living room was removed. It is not stretching the point to say that Wright placed some Japanese influence in this cottage design. What was once a one-bedroom, one-bath cottage has grown now to three bedrooms and two baths. The expansive projected roof over the front entrance might just be Wright's most welcoming, uncomplicated entryway.

SHERMAN M. BOOTH HOUSE

Address: 265 Sylvan Road, Glencoe, Illinois

Built: 1915

Sherman Booth became a part of Frank Lloyd Wright's life at a critical juncture, a time in which he needed a good attorney. The two shared nearby offices in Chicago for a time. Booth provided Wright with legal representation and financial advice, neither of which Wright took too seriously. But, in addition to a commission for a small bungalow designed for Booth and his wife, Elizabeth, in 1911, as a honeymoon cottage, Wright also designed this stately residence as a dwelling for his attorney. Booth eventually went on to develop a series of Wright homes constructed in the wild environs and leafy geography of Glencoe, just thirty miles up the lakefront, north of Chicago. Glencoe boasts the third-largest collection of Wright homes with nine in all in the suburb.

Booth was also the brother of Mrs. Herbert Angster, for whom Wright designed a residence (now demolished) in nearby Lake Bluff in 1911. The house that was eventually built here for Booth was not Wright's first design. An earlier plan on a much grander scale, calling for some remarkably excessive architectural features, not least of which was an entrance bridge spanning a ravine, had to be abandoned to fit the financial resources of the client. The anticipated cost proved too much for Booth, who was able to have the architect simplify both the cost and the proposed proportions of the design.

The result was this flat-roofed, three-story stucco and timber cube with a connecting one-story, rectangular brick projection and a low, hipped

Right: The Sherman Booth House is Wright's anchor for the Ravine Bluffs Development, a house with Prairie character, geometric massing, wide roof projections, and horizontal banding.

Left: Fashioned of concrete, a favored material of the architect, an outdoor lamp of Wright's at the Sherman Booth House has Prairie-style simplicity.

Above: The Sherman Booth House viewed from the air permits the full drama of its Prairie massing and almost geometrically cubical form to be fully appreciated.

roof. Booth consented to a $16,000 budget for the house, a price that was most economical and far below the $60,000 price tag of the Robie House. Wright had previously designed a barn and a gardener's cottage on the large property owned by the Booths. When he created the Booths' new house, Wright incorporated the two previous structures within the design of the new structure. The final product was a four-story central block with the barn refashioned into the south wing and the gardener's cottage remade as the eastern bedroom wing. Low, hipped roofs extend on the two wings. The central block has a flat roof. The chimney rises at the juncture of the cube and the two rectangular wings. This strange combination gives the house dramatic lift and centers its axis.

Wright's use of such geometric shapes produced a powerfully modern-looking house, a mature Prairie-style design. On the top floor, the flat roof of the cube contains a garden and a screened porch with its own hearth. Wright added distinction to the house by his attention to such design features as the broad overhangs that extend with shade and shelter at each level of the structure. Some of his most superb furniture was built for the Booth House, such as the Prairie-style canopy beds in the master bedroom, as well as built-in closets and specially designed floor lamps. Little is left of the dining-room table and chairs that were an important feature in the house. The public rooms were designed on a grand scale, with the living room measuring some thirty-six feet in length. This house became an anchor for further Wright designs in Glencoe. Booth's interest in the revolutionary new style introduced by Wright extended the architect's use of the form for a period. Wright, however, had already left the Prairie style behind him, advancing to new levels of expression. This house and the other homes of Booth's Ravine Bluffs Development are sandwiched between two of Wright's most significant commercial projects, the Midway Gardens in Chicago (1913) and the Imperial Hotel in Tokyo (1915), both now demolished. The Booth House is one of Wright's last large Prairie designs.

CHARLES R. PERRY HOUSE, RAVINE BLUFFS DEVELOPMENT

Address: 272 Sylvan Road, Glencoe, Illinois
Built: 1915

Wright's subdivision designs for Sherman Booth are really a misnomer. The concept of a subdivision in woodsy Glencoe along the Lake Michigan shoreline is not the usual, predictable cookie-cutter domestic neighborhood. The abundance of rich and effusive nature erases any connection with the characteristics of other typical American subdivisions. Glencoe's affluence and natural abundance of nature's potency removes any such fear of that. Wright placed his Prairie residences of the Ravine Bluffs Development within the context of this extraordinary geological and historical phenomenon. This was terrain that was once thick with the Potawatomis, the native people who made their home along the waterways of northern Illinois. The site provided a stunning wooded geography more complex than the plain upon which his Oak Park and River Forest homes sat. When the Chicago and Northwestern Railroad made Glencoe a regular stop, Chicago was just a newspaper read away. It was in this that Wright agreed to fashion his Prairie-style neighborhood. Each of these five homes was designed as a square-plan house, providing a pragmatic and utilitarian form to interior living.

The anchor within each dwelling is the central fireplace, in a living room encompassing half of the first floor. A porch extends this area further. The kitchen and dining room complete the plan for the first floor. The second level contains three bedrooms, a bathroom, and an upstairs porch, perfect for summer sleeping. The exterior cladding has Wright's familiar stucco. Strong horizontal framing is provided by the banding that begins at the base. It continues across the area beneath the windowsills and then is reinforced by the powerful lines created by the unusual roof design. The Perry House is made unique from its mates by the addition of gables inserted within the cornice of the flat roofline. The extensive, cantilevered projection of the entry roof is reminiscent of Wright's Chicago "pagoda house" for Judge Foster. The gable becomes a central design feature here above the entryway, deep, inviting, and sheltered by its wide sweep. It provides the house with an exotic character and a touch of Asian artistry that is evocative, like the Hills-DeCaro House in Oak Park. The roof at the Perry House makes a dramatic statement and imbues it with a special individuality among Wright's other Glencoe designs. A broad, low chimney sits midroof, a telltale emblem of its cozy Prairie-style interior.

Right: Wright achieved a special note of individuality among the homes of the Ravine Bluffs Development by the variety of roof designs used. Here at the Perry House, it is the angularity of the gabling in the roof that distinguishes it.

HOLLIS R. ROOT HOUSE, RAVINE BLUFFS DEVELOPMENT

Address: 1030 Meadow
Road, Glencoe, Illinois
Built: 1915

It is hard to believe that the Hollis R. Root House is roughly the same house as the Perry House in this Wright development in Glencoe. What really sets these two homes apart is their roofs. Wright gave the Root House an even more horizontal character. It provides the house, on a smaller scale, with that unmistakable profile so familiar in his flat-roofed masterpieces, the Tomek House, the Robie House, and the Balch House. The same interior plan unfolds as in the Root House. Half the area of the first floor is taken up with the living room, facing the central hearth. This area is enlarged by the contiguous porch, now enclosed, that adds spaciousness and proportion. The remaining area of the first floor is split between the kitchen and the dining room.

Three bedrooms and a bathroom were part of the original second-floor design. Contemporary renovation has refashioned the rooms into a spacious library and single bedroom. The flat rooflines and projecting side roofs give the house a strong linear character. The exterior is of stucco with continuous banding at the base and beneath the windowsills on both the first and second floors. The geometric expression of the house is enlarged by the rectangular

Left: The flat roofline of the Hollis Root House is another example of Wright's willingness to build variety into his design of the Ravine Bluffs Development.

verticality of the windows throughout. The unusual landscape of Glencoe provided a setting in which Wright could fashion modest, but architecturally significant dwellings. The central block of the house has a decidedly Cubic character that is reinforced by the lower roof's horizontal sweep. The lintel above the central windows contributes to the horizontal sight line.

The main entranceway at the Root House is surprisingly uncomplicated and obvious, with simple stairs and a doorway easily seen at the right end of the façade. More expansive than the Hunt House in LaGrange, the Root House is similar to the "Fireproof House for $5,000" that first appeared in the *Ladies' Home Journal* (April 1907). Wright had already moved away from the design of Prairie-style dwellings when he consented to provide Sherman Booth with these homes. Some critics believe his finest moments in Prairie-designed dwellings were behind him and that this development was a step backward for Wright. Glencoe, however, remains second only to Oak Park among the suburbs of Chicago for its number of Wright-designed houses. There are nine in all. Among the many historical homes and gracious mansions of Glencoe, Wright enjoys an unusual local prominence. He brought a fresh, modern expression to a terrain of uncontroverted beauty.

Right: An aerial view of the Hollis Root House displays its classic Prairie cruciform plan, as well as its unique setting surrounded by lush natural woodland.

WILLIAM F. KIER HOUSE, RAVINE BLUFFS DEVELOPMENT

Address: 1031 Meadow Road, Glencoe, Illinois

Built: 1915

Unlike some of Wright's other, more dramatic designs, the architect did not preside over the actual construction phase of the homes in the Ravine Bluffs Development project. He took little interest in the details of what was unfolding. Sandwiched between the elaborate commercial achievements of the Midway Garden in Chicago and the Imperial Hotel in Tokyo, this enormous Glencoe project was done as more of a favor to Sherman Booth than anything else. Here in the Kier House, Wright demonstrated his unique ability to fashion architecture deep in nature and at the same time provide sturdy utility in scale and aesthetics.

The roof of the Kier House is hipped in the strongest of Prairie traditions. As a companion design to the Perry House, it sits with grandeur and a pristine majesty in the heart of a lush, wooded ravine. Sherman Booth's brother-in-law Herbert Angster was actually its first owner. This was not their first home by the architect, for Wright had previously designed a house for the Angsters in nearby Lake Bluff in 1911. Little information, however, survives about William and Eva Kier, who were actually the second owners. Further confusion is at hand when the house is additionally referred to as the Ellis House, after yet another early owner. The house sits on a third of an acre surrounded by lush natural beauty, an outgrowth of the deeply forested ravine that first inspired the development of this unique Wright community. The low, hipped roof tapers with an expansive flare along its eaves, providing shelter and an exotic roofline that is reminiscent of the Hills House's Asian beauty. Rich horizontal lines are evocative of the true Wrightian Prairie style here. Generous banding carries out that refining horizontal line, as do the rooflines on each floor. The application of the hipped roof on this house lowers the verticality that is achieved by the flat roof on the Root House.

The familiar central chimney, broad and narrow, is another powerful Prairie component. Graceful variety is established among the five Ravine Bluffs houses that belie their inherent square-plan

Above: The Kier House is an example of sturdy utility in scale and aesthetics.

Above: **An essentially square-plan house, the Kier House is topped by a hipped roof.**

similarity and footprint kinship. The roof here also lends itself to furthering the square profile of the structure. The variety in window treatments shows the individuality among these Ravine Bluffs houses. Here in the Kier House, graceful latticework glazing along the second-floor windows expresses such variety. The Kier House is most significantly varied from the other Wright houses within this development by its rotation of ninety degrees in its relationship to the street. This permits an optimal exposure to natural light during the day with the living room having a southern exposure. The porte cochere once had a profile that was born in the veranda of the Tomek House—an expansive roof plate, supported by strong vertical massing, created a stately entrance with both power and depth, projecting a pavilionlike structure that was in harmony with the overall angularity of the house. The original design, however, has been altered by opening up the low walls to permit driveway access to the garage. Throughout the Ravine Bluffs project, Wright created homes with a sense of variety without ever having to alter the basic design of the structures. In addition to the three square-plan homes included here, two more were constructed, the Ross House and the Kissam House. Together with the Sherman Booth House, they make up the six houses of the Ravine Bluffs Development.

WILLIAM F. ROSS HOUSE, RAVINE BLUFFS DEVELOPMENT

Address: 1027 Meadow Road, Glencoe, Illinois
Built: 1915

The Ross House is a part of Wright's attorney-friend Sherman Booth's Ravine Bluffs Development that he designed just before his last Chicago design, the Bach House (1915) and his relocation to Japan for the building of the Imperial Hotel (1916). The homes that Booth built here in the North Shore suburb of Glencoe were originally meant to be rental property. The Ross House, together with its nearby neighbors on Meadow Road, all blend into the rich wooded landscape with a soft and easy comfort. Wright was intrigued by the beauty and natural environment that Glencoe offered early in the twentieth century. Its nearness to the drama of Lake Michigan and its unique woodland character provided the architect with the kind of honest, organic setting from which his designs could emerge.

Like its neighbors, the Ross House is a Prairie dwelling with a stucco exterior, a hipped roof, deep-set overhanging eaves, and basic square-plan interiors. The Ross House is the variation of that interior. The special placement of the fireplace to serve as a feature of the entryway realigns the flow of the first floor here. The veranda, originally open, is now enclosed. The living room accesses the veranda and the dining room is set to the rear with the kitchen to the side. The house has four bedrooms. The Booth plan for Glencoe had originality and creative intelligence, bringing Wright's remarkable Prairie aesthetics to an area on the edge of development. It offered fine structures in an avant-garde mode that many residents found to be appealing. Wright's homes continue to define the aesthetics of Glencoe and have earned much respect for the architect. Today, their designs are still fresh, made more mellow by time and familiarity.

DANIEL AND LUTE KISSAM HOUSE, RAVINE BLUFFS DEVELOPMENT

Address: 1023 Meadow Road,
Glencoe, Illinois
Built: 1915

The flat roof and deep, overhanging edge of the Kissam House is expressive of the simplicity that Wright breathed into his Ravine Bluffs Development homes. Designed in 1915, the crisp, horizontal lines of the Kissam House can easily be seen in the Bach House, Wright's last Chicago-designed house. Though fashioned of distinctly different materials, each house demonstrates Wright's Prairie aesthetic for flat, uncomplicated projecting planes. A subtle Asian sensibility is also apparent in the clean lines and unembellished stucco and wood house with dramatic horizontal banding that sets the tone of its Prairie mystique. The Kissam House, like its other Meadow Road neighbors, adheres to a basic square plan of large living room, dining room, and kitchen anchored by the central living room hearth. The houses of the Ravine Bluffs Development all share a common floor plan, but significant variations in their exterior modifications provide them with their own unique individuality. Alterations in the style of roof or the way in which the house sits in its lot allow each structure a certain amount of complementary style. The Kissam House appears visually distinct from its neighbors in large part by its rotation on the property. Similarities with the Hollis Root House are only fully appreciated upon a close inspection because the Kissam House is rotated ninety degrees on its property. Wright's willingness to take advantage of the pristine woodland setting and his singular ability to fashion a dwelling of elegant modernity to fit the setting is a triumph.

Left: The flat rooflines of the Kissam House demonstrate the variety that was a part of the Ravine Bluffs Development. Exterior stucco and wood cladding and horizontal banding reinforce the Prairie design.

RAVINE BLUFFS BRIDGE AND SCULPTURES, RAVINE BLUFFS DEVELOPMENT

Address: Sylvan Road, Glencoe, Illinois
Built: 1915

These important design features, a bridge and sculptures, bring an expansive sense of unity to Wright's subdivision for Sherman Booth, as well as fulfilling important functions in this rocky geography. This may be Wright's most curious terrain preceding his Fallingwater masterpiece in Mill Run, Pennsylvania, in 1938. The land surrounding these Glencoe homes is as rough as it is bounteous of nature. This bridge, one of only two freestanding bridges ever designed by Wright, serves an important purpose in spanning the cavern of a rocky ravine. It makes public access to the development possible and accomplishes this in the best of Prairie traditions. The bridge is located at the northeast gateway to the development project along Sylvan Road. A remarkable horizontal character is the bridge's most defining design feature. This is established by the introduction of low, poured-concrete walls that provide pedestrians with a built-in place to sit. The geometry of these tablelike structures is reminiscent of the flat profile of the Unity Temple in Oak Park, also fashioned in poured concrete. Midway Gardens in Chicago, which preceded the Ravine Bluffs designs, was also a poured concrete structure of coolly decorative form. Its nearness in time to the Glencoe project made it a natural influence on both the bridge and sculptures.

The close-to-the-ground overall height of the bridge obscures nothing in nature. Tall, square, cubelike pillars are fitted with lamps wrought in copper. Wright blended in design features from many past projects here with small subtleties. The concrete itself provides Wright with a pliable substance with which to sculpt this very modern bridge. Three sculptures, also of cast concrete, are included in the development and serve, ultimately, as a utilitarian feature marking the boundaries of the Booth development's perimeters. The sculptures are very geometric—concrete cubes, rectangles, and spheres assembled at right angles to each other. The spheres are very similar to Wright's beach ball–like vases wrought in copper that were a part of several early Prairie houses. Today they are very rare and fetch high prices at auction near the half-million-dollar range. The shapes in the three sculptures are elementary and basic and here are about movement toward perfection, the accomplishment of Wright's organic design. Copper plates identify the "Ravine Bluffs." One is located at the west end of Sylvan Road, another is at Franklin Road at Meadow, and the third is at the east end of Sylvan Road. Both the bridge and two of the sculptures have been rebuilt following long years of exposure to the severity of lakeside winters. Most importantly, the bridge and sculptures provided Wright with a way of etching his name and character across a significant face of rugged terrain.

Above: Wright's design for the Ravine Bluffs Development includes this low-rise, Prairie-style bridge fashioned of poured concrete.

Right: The Ravine Bluffs Bridge has Prairie-style urns and lamps.

Far right: Wright created three spherical concrete sculptures to mark the boundaries of the development's perimeters.

EDMUND D. BRIGHAM HOUSE

Address: 790 Sheridan Road,
Glencoe, Illinois
Built: 1915

Wright designed the Brigham House the year before his eventful escape to Europe with Mrs. Cheney, though it was not built until 1915, the year he fashioned so many Glencoe homes for Sherman Booth. This house is not a part of that Ravine Bluffs Development plan. Edmund D. Brigham was an executive of the Chicago and Northwestern Railroad, which served particularly Chicago's North Shore suburbs. The rail line made it possible for businessmen with offices in Chicago to have spacious lakeside homes that were no more than a thirty-minute commute. In the Brigham House, it is easy to see the familiar shadow of Wright's "Fireproof House for $5,000" at the center of the structure. The squarish massing and graceful roofline projections of the Hunt House (1907) in LaGrange and the Stockman House (1908) have a similar look. The Evans House (1908) in Chicago follows a similar beginning—a two-story central block expanded by two one-story wings.

What makes the Brigham House unique is that Wright designed the house in concrete. The architect came to have a profound respect and delight for concrete through his experience in designing the Unity Temple in Oak Park in 1904. Concrete's pliability and durability had important modern aesthetics for Wright that went beyond his reliance on plaster stucco. He said that it was "mechanically perfect." Concrete had deep artistic dimensions for him and he relished the ways in which it could be shaped and sculptured. Its freshness intrigued Wright and added architectural drama (the walls are twenty-two inches thick) to his design for the Brigham House, the only Prairie domestic residence he built in concrete. The hipped roof, expansive projecting overhangs, horizontal banding, and central chimney block are all traditional Wright Prairie features. Symmetry and proportion mark the essential architectural plan of this house, rich in understated elegance. This is a well-maintained Prairie treasure that fits well into the wooded scented landscape of Glencoe.

Right: **The hearth takes center stage in the living room of the Brigham House, a typical feature of Wright's architectural designs.**

1916

J. J. O'CONNOR HOUSE, AMERICAN SYSTEMS-BUILT BUNGALOW

Address: 330 Gregory Street, Wilmette, Illinois
Built: 1916

Above: A strong sense of symmetry is achieved in this single-story, American Systems-Built Bungalow, whose Prairie-style pedigree is strengthened by Wright's ribbon of windows across the façade.

This handsome, cozy one-story bungalow in the North Shore suburb of Wilmette represented a new extension of Frank Lloyd Wright into the market of American housing. Though these houses were actually designed by the architect, the client was not the eventual homebuyer, but rather the builder or fabricator who purchased the plans from Wright. During the construction phase, Wright had no influence on the building of the structures. The homeowner dealt only with the construction company, never Wright himself. Remarkably, the very strong shadow of the architect is pronounced in these modest, affordable family homes. The buyer received quality and great value. Though not as aesthetically revolutionary as Wright's singular Prairie mansions in Oak Park or River Forest, each of the American Systems-Built homes had their own revolutionary characters, made possible by the prefabrication of design modules that were made to Wright's specifications. Arthur R. Richards of the American Realty Service Company was responsible for their construction in both the Chicago and Milwaukee areas. Wright's Prairie imprint deeply wraps each Systems-Built structure.

Here in tony Wilmette, the O'Connor House joins the Baker House as one of Wright's two homes in that lakefront suburb. This is a comfortable house, with a gracefully sloping, hipped roof. Deep eaves extend with familiar Wright shade and shelter. The anchoring of the house at the axis of the central chimney repeats a

constant of the Wright form. Exterior cladding in stucco is a design refrain that reinforces the true Prairie form of this structure. The proportion of the house is well balanced. Though built on a larger scale than the Coonley Gardner's Cottage, vestiges of that tiny house can be seen in this wisteria-clad bungalow. Exterior gardens now surround the house and wrap it in a rich, natural, botanical splendor. The soft, gingerbread-like patina is unusual for a Wright dwelling.

The house sits low to the ground, a perspective that is deepened by the low rise of the roof and its overhang. Windows wrap the corners of the house and provide remarkable natural light across the interior. The dark framing and extensive linear banding beneath the windowsills and above the foundation increases the horizontal expression of the structure. The O'Connor House is a good expression of the new genre in domestic design by Wright that is easily fabricated, easily maintained, and easily affordable. Another expression of this one-story bungalow design was built in Lake Bluff, a suburb further up the lakefront just past Lake Forest. It is known as the William J. Vanderkloot House and has become more weathered by the elements through the years.

WILLIAM J. VANDERKLOOT HOUSE, AMERICAN SYSTEMS-BUILT BUNGALOW

Address: 231 Prospect Avenue, Lake Bluff, Illinois
Built: 1916

Located along the Lake Michigan shoreline, just north of Lake Forest, Lake Bluff has always been a quiet, leafy piece of aristocratic geography, the camping grounds of branches of the McCormicks, the Armours, and other quiet fortunes. At one time, Harold McCormick purchased some 250 acres of prime land and engaged Frank Lloyd Wright to design a lakeside retreat. Mrs. McCormick—Edith Rockefeller, the daughter of John D. himself—quickly put an end to those plans because of her dislike of Wright, thus depriving Lake Bluff of what might have been a Wright masterpiece. Wright's great Prairie house designed for Herbert Angster in 1911 has been demolished. So here in Lake Bluff, thick with rare designs by David Adler, Wright's only standing structure is this one-story bungalow, designed for Arthur L. Richard's American Systems-Built homes. The house was built for William J. Vanderkloot as an investment, just down the street from his own house. Vanderkloot's family were the barons of the Chicago iron industry, stretching from steelworks to ornamental fabrication. Among their holdings was the Chicago Ornamental Iron Company, the firm that fashioned Louis Sullivan's elaborate botanical iron ornamentation of the Carson Pirie Scott Department Store in Chicago. Wright would have been familiar with their artistic capabilities from his days with Sullivan. As a single-story Systems-Built structure, it has many similarities with the J. J. O'Connor House in Wilmette. Its hipped roof, deeply projecting overhangs, and simple cottage form were symbols of Wright's attempt to provide architectural quality, as well as economy, an elusive dream toward which he would work all his life. Vanderkloot quickly sold the house to Ida and Grace McElwain, sisters who lived in the house for many years. This bungalow was built for modernity, simplicity, and ease.

Left: Wright set the windows at right angles to each other in the corners of this American Systems-Built single-story bungalow and added extensive projection in the eaves of the low-sloping, hipped roof.

OSCAR A. JOHNSON HOUSE (HANNEY & SON HOUSE), AMERICAN SYSTEMS-BUILT TWO-STORY HOUSE

Address: 2614 Lincolnwood Drive, Evanston, Illinois
Built: 1916

The Oscar A. Johnson House in the North Shore suburb of Evanston is a neighbor of the O'Connor Bungalow in Wilmette. This two-story American Systems-Built house demonstrates the variety that was a part of the prefabricated catalog. The Johnson House has a strong cubic character—far more geometric than those that followed. Though it lacks the handy addition of the porte cochere and enclosed porch of the Smith House on Chicago's South Side, there are powerful points of commonality. The central placement of the rectangular window sets on the façades of both the first and second stories is a common thread in each. Both also have prominent front entrances, an unusual feature in a Wright house. The exterior cladding is stucco and wood, a point of unity between all of these designs.

The Johnson House has a strong verticality, but the horizontal character of the structure is softly echoed in the banding that stretches across the upper area of the house above the top framing of the upper windows. That horizontal line is echoed in the window framing in which the sill and lintel deepen the shape of the windows. This is a feature shared by each of the two-story American Systems-Built houses. Above the rectangular entryway, single windows set one above the other create a strong vertical line that accentuates the geometric tension. The hipped roof has a gentle slope with extending overhangs that are modest in their reach. The versatility of this design, "plasticality" in Wright's vernacular, demonstrates the variety available to customers. The Johnson House is a version of the Smith Model House without the porte cochere and enclosed second-story porch. It is the cube without the wing. Handsome and very practical, it is said that the original budget for this house was $4,000, a tighter economy than others of this genre. But the final product is fresh, modern, and decisively innovative. This house is light-years ahead of many of its contemporary dwellings.

There is little in the way of external ornamentation, a fact that heightens the simplicity of the structure's overall geometry. Wright was refashioning domestic architecture in these Systems-Built designs. Modest homes for the upper middle class was his goal in which the quality of regular houses was expanded by Wright's commitment to innovative designs, particularly within. Rooms were no longer

Right: The two-story Oscar A. Johnson House was built for utility and economy, reflecting Wright's imperative to fashion domestic dwellings that were affordable. Its stucco and wood façade is emblematic of Wright's Prairie style.

Above: Upper windows at the Oscar A. Johnson House are set at right angles to each other, providing the fullest infusion of natural light into bedrooms.

Left: Deep-set overhanging eaves, horizontal banding, and tall, rectangular window sets exemplify the Wright design aesthetic.

designed as little boxes; instead the architect opened up the interior and created a plan in which rooms flowed one into the other. While this concept is prevalent in domestic architecture today, it was revolutionary in the early decades of the twentieth century. Wright unleashed this revolution on the American family, making it possible for them to enjoy domestic designs that provided quality and innovation at the most economical of costs. Wright was expanding the horizons of the American family with these designs. The firm of Hanney and Son constructed this particular house and the present owner notes that no others of this basic design were built. Houses in the prefabricated designs were constructed by the American Systems-Built Company in Gary, Indiana; Milwaukee, Wisconsin; and Monona, Iowa.

1917

H. HOWARD HYDE HOUSE, AMERICAN SYSTEMS-BUILT TWO-STORY HOUSE

Address: 10541 S. Hoyne Avenue, Chicago, Illinois
Built: 1917

The H. Howard Hyde House in Chicago's Beverly Hills neighborhood is one of two American Systems-Built homes in the city. Located within one block of each other, they were originally constructed for a larger-scale development for a subdivision known then as the "Ridge Homes." They were to be part of a larger community of similar houses planned for access to the nearby golf course at Ridge Country Club. The area is contiguous to a natural geological ridge along the Kettle Morraine plateau. While Wright's theory of affordable housing was aimed at providing architecturally significant modern dwellings at modest prices, the target audience was hardly lower-income. The American System-Built designs were essentially for upper-middle-class home buyers. Of the two houses constructed on Hoyne Avenue, one was built as a model home for inspection by prospective clients. The other, built here for H. Howard Hyde, a financial officer of the International Harvester Company, was ordered directly from the American Systems-Built catalog in early 1917. It has some similarities to its neighbors, but it is the mirror image of the Delbert W. Meier House in Monona, Iowa.

Not including the price of the land, these houses could be built for about $6,000, a respectable value for the quality. Selecting from the catalog provided certain variety and more individuality. The architectural key to the Hyde House is the way Wright was able to "break the box," that is, the ability of the architect to fashion a floor plan that departed from the usual footprint of boxlike rooms. He had demonstrated this concept of "open rooms," flowing one into the other in some of his most important

Left: **Wright's H. H. Hyde House has extensive horizontal banding along its stucco façade. The architect set the windows at right angles in the corners in this two-story American Systems-Built house.**

Prairie designs in Oak Park and River Forest. In Chicago, the Robie House is his most stunning example. Here, he is able to translate that feature into more modestly proportioned and economically priced family dwellings.

The Hyde House incorporates many of the same features in Wright's early Prairie-style houses. Exterior cladding is stucco and wood. Generous banding across the façade extends the horizontal character that is found on so many of the architect's residential structures. A broad, sloping, hipped roof extends with generous, expansive overhangs. A wide central chimney establishes the central feature of the interior anchor, the hearth of handsome, narrow Roman brick. Until recently, this brickwork, one of Wright's signature features, was concealed behind a plaster covering. A hidden opening allows fireplace ash to be sent by a shoot to a trap down in the home's full basement. Eighty-eight vertically rectangular windows on both the first and second floors maximize the infusion of natural light into the home's interior. The main entryway is set away from sight, concealed along the north side of the house. A stucco entry frames the stairs with deep sheltering. On the street side of Hoyne Avenue, facing south, first-floor windows are in sets at both the center of the living room and in a small study near the entryway that extends into the living room area. Along the south and east walls, multiple sets of windows frame the dining room that flows from the living room. Second-floor windows are joined at right angles at the corners. The present owners have restored this Chicago landmark to exacting specifications. Its original glory shines again, demonstrating Wright's concept of genteel domesticity imaginatively designed.

Above: The handsome hipped roof on the garage provides extended roof edges. The flower box brings nature ever closer.

Right: Deep, projecting roof overhangs provide practical shelter above the side entryway that shields the main entrance from the street.

Far left: A refined art-glass window in the Hyde House filters an abundance of natural light into the hallway of the home.

Left: The central hearth of the Hyde House was encased in plaster that concealed the elegant Roman brick design until recent renovation uncovered its hidden angular beauty.

GUY C. SMITH HOUSE, AMERICAN SYSTEMS-BUILT TWO-STORY HOUSE

Address: 10410 S. Hoyne Avenue, Chicago, Illinois
Built: 1917

Recent ongoing renovation is also the main feature of the second American Systems-Built design in Chicago. It, too, is in the Beverly Hills neighborhood on the city's South Side. The Guy C. Smith House was the design model constructed for the "Ridge Homes." There are a number of substantial differences between this house and the neighboring Hyde House on the next block. The addition of the porte cochere with its second-story enclosed porch with a hipped roof is one glaring design alteration. The porch is bright with natural light and adds a convenient extension of usable interior space. Exterior stucco and cypress cladding has been carefully restored and provides a fresh complement to the structure. A low-rise hipped roof with deep overhangs and a broad, central brick chimney are familiar Wright design features. At the back end of the house on the second floor, beside the porch of the porte cochere, is a maid's bathroom containing the most unusual design feature in a Wright house, the cantilevered bathtub. A central planter box across the façade, beneath the first-floor sill, is another familiar Wright detail. Narrow, vertically rectangular windows at each level provide the interior with expansive natural light. The entryway is central and visible in the façade with convenient access to the driveway, without the complicated features many Wright entries thrive on.

The real key elements of Wright's genius are, however, on the interior. Fine woods are in abundance, a thoughtful feature of a design model. Birch is throughout—light, bright, and handsome, it creates an interior that is one of the most pleasant in any Wright-designed home. This wood is carried through the house and is used with particular effect on the second story, where built-in cabinets and a built-in window seat off the porch are important vintage expressions of Wright's hand.

Right: The Guy Smith House is an American Systems-Built home that features a porte cochere and upper-level room over the driveway, similar to the Heisen House in Villa Park.

Rooms are flowing and open, another of Wright's "break-the-box" designs. This floorplan of rooms opening into each other provides a most modern and efficient utility. Present owners have engaged in significant restoration of this Chicago landmark. Interior walls are bright in light Prairie colors that enhance the elegance of the birch wood. Like other American Systems-Built homes of Wright, this one was only discovered by Tim Samuelson of the Chicago Landmarks Commission in 1990. Ironically, Wright's ready-cut designs were to be about providing affordable housing. Today, however, the present owners are major investors in the constant upkeep that ensures the architect's most treasured features remain in pristine condition. The present owners of the Smith house consider it an act of devotion to the spirit of the architect, having a wide vocabulary in all the nuances and peculiarities of living in a Wright landmark. This is a house of grace and patience, where "affordable" carries a new definition.

Above: Wright's extensive use of birch wood in built-in cabinets adds a warm, glowing shimmer, particularly throughout the second-floor hallway and bedrooms.

Left: The dining room of the Guy Smith House is bright with massive amounts of interior light from the ribbon of windows that are characteristic of Wright's American Systems-Built designs.

Above: Wright included a small built-in bench beneath these windows on the second-floor landing just outside the room above the porte cochere.

CHARLES HEISEN HOUSE, AMERICAN SYSTEMS-BUILT TWO-STORY HOUSE

Address: 346 Highland Avenue, Villa Park, Illinois
Built: 1917

This is Illinois' latest Wright discovery. The young homeowners were still fresh from their wedding, like other Wright residents before them over the decades, when they were alerted to the Wright pedigree of their home by a

savvy Wright aficionado who lived nearby. The two-story American Systems-Built home sits on an expansive corner lot. In many ways it resembles its architecturally genetic kin, the Smith House. In an apparent variation on that model, the Heisen House has its main entrance on the opposite, south end of the house. Two more separate private entrances, more readily accessible, are within the porte cochere and second-story enclosed porch on the north side, as well as at the rear of the kitchen. The porch and driveway opening are set back more deeply here than at the Smith House. The graceful, hipped roof and expansive, deep overhangs are more generous here than at the Smith House, with a more defined angularity.

Below: The Charles Heisen House is a recently discovered Wright design, a two-story American Systems-Built home in which the architect struggled to make his designs economically affordable, as well as aesthetically pleasing.

Top: Stucco and wood exterior cladding is an essential component of Wright's American Systems-Built homes, originally devised as his "Fireproof House for $5,000."

Above: Graceful, sloping hipped roofs flow into generous, extended eaves in Wright's Heisen House.

Right: The Heisen House has a handsome porte cochere with an upper-level room above the driveway. Extensive roof projections provide protection to the exterior stucco cladding.

Generous windows in sets sweep across the façade and around the house, expanding the use of natural light within the interior. So prominent was this fresh exposure that the house was advertised as "a bright, cheerful home."

The main entryway brings people through a large, deep-set entrance foyer, with the living room stretched across the width of the central façade to the right. To the left, a spacious dining room flows unbroken in this open plan. The kitchen, large by Wright proportions, is accessed behind the dining area. A central hearth anchors the living room. A central staircase, broad and far more open than Wright's usual style, leads up directly from the hall. At the half level, the enclosed porch, above the porte cochere, is easily accessed. On the next level, bedrooms are expansive, with a second fireplace in the master bedroom. The exterior is clad in stucco with cypress trim, the dominant Prairie materials in these houses.

Heisen is said to have been a property developer in Chicago's business community. He recognized the great value that the American Systems-Built houses demonstrated. As a man of real estate, he easily would have been familiar with the newspaper advertisements that appeared about the houses, written by famed American writer Sherwood Anderson. Villa Park was a countrylike village then, set in the western suburbs of Chicago, directly west of Oak Park and River Forest. If Heisen had seen the newspaper ads, he would have recognized a model very similar to the one that he purchased. Customers were encouraged to select a plan that they liked "designed by America's great creative architect." More than anything else, the utility and the modernity of the design were characterized as that of an "American Home," a home emblematic of national ideals and sensible economics, distinguished by its innovation and quality of design and craftsmanship. Long before prefabrication was a staple of American housing construction, Wright's partnership with the American Systems-Built concept was revolutionizing what was possible to achieve in domestic home design. The project might have seen more success but for the great slump in the housing market with the advent of World War I. It would be almost a half century before the concept of prefabrication would be back, becoming a necessity in the boom in the market following World War II.

FRANK LLOYD WRIGHT'S LIFE 1910–1919

Wright returned from Europe at the end of 1910 and ushered in further personal discomfort. He reentered the family home in Oak Park and turned the key in the door of the studio, attempting to rebuild his architectural practice. Ever the modern realist, he knew he could not continue long under that roof. His mother, delighting in the troubles faced by her daughter-in-law, Catherine, gifted her son with some two hundred acres of rolling countryside near Spring Green, Wisconsin, with the thought that he could build a suitable home for himself in a new life away from Oak Park. Wright developed this land in the years ahead into what became his beloved Taliesin, named for the Celtic bard who sang the praises of architecture and art at the court of King Arthur. Over the course of the decade, he would design close to sixty buildings of extraordinary modernity. In addition to the design and construction of his new Wisconsin home and architectural center, he continued to create buildings of singular architectural importance, among which were the Adams House (1913), the last of his Oak Park designs; some expansive commercial enterprises, including the Midway Gardens (1913), a lavish Chicago beer garden; the Ravine Bluffs Development project (1915) in Glencoe, Illinois, commissioned by his attorney Sherman Booth; the American Systems-Built Homes, a prefabricated line of dwellings commissioned by builder Arthur L. Richards; the extraordinary Imperial Hotel in Tokyo, Japan (1915–1919), that brought remarkable international notoriety to Wright; and the Emil Bach House (1915), his last residential design executed in the city of Chicago.

This was the period of some of Wright's greatest personal triumphs. His ability to get his career moving again demonstrates the significance of his architectural reputation that even his relationship with Mamah Borthwick Cheney could not wreck. However, it is also a time marked with some of his most horrific personal tragedies. Taliesin, in the green valley of the Lloyd Joneses, became his lifeboat. He and Mamah Borthwick Cheney escaped there, back amid the Wisconsin countryside of his origins, and fashioned a hideaway that would grow into an architectural studio, retreat, and fortress. In the summer of 1914, while Wright was lost in the details of the construction of the Midway Gardens project and the world tumbled into the catastrophe of World War I, Mamah Borthwick Cheney entertained her two children at Taliesin. On the afternoon of August 14, Julian Carleton, the cook at Taliesin, went berserk, set fire to Taliesin, and murdered seven people, including Mamah Borthwick Cheney; her two children; Emil Brodelle, a young architectural apprentice; thirteen-year-old Ernest Weston, a worker's son; and two workers, Thomas Brunker and David

Right: Olgivanna Ivanovna Lazovich Wright (center) with the architect and their daughter Iovanna. The financial demands of his second wife and the virulent press attacks forced Wright to go into hiding with Olgivanna when they first met. He eventually married her and lived with her for the rest of his life.

Lindblom. Tragedy was compounded by tragedy. Wright's great love was dead and his beloved Taliesin lay in ruins. Wright buried her on the grounds of Taliesin. He was inconsolable.

Wright's interest in designing his series of one-story and two-story Prairie-style homes for Arthur L. Richards's American Systems-Built project demonstrates an important ongoing element within Wright's work. He was relentless in attempting to fashion a house that would be both architecturally significant and economical. Bringing housing of substance to the masses was more than a clever exercise, it was part of Wright's larger sense of American democracy. The failure of these houses to flourish is tied to the entry of the United States in the war and the subsequent drop in the housing market related to the wartime economy. Wright, however, would not be deterred. He spent the remainder of the decade out of the country, working onsite in Tokyo with the construction of the Imperial Hotel and its 1919 annex. From 1916 until 1922, Wright lived in Japan, absorbing a culture for which he had a long affinity. The influence of Japanese art on some of his previous designs was always palpable. He was afforded both living quarters and a studio in the new hotel that boasted some of the most inventive technologies of the age. His floating foundation was an architectural marvel. Together with his steel frame construction, each was highly praised when an earthquake destroyed much of Tokyo in 1923 and the Imperial Hotel remained standing. Wright would amplify the influence of Japanese aesthetics in his later works.

Above: The Imperial Hotel, Tokyo, as it appeared in 1958. It survived the earthquake of 1923 that destroyed most of Tokyo.

Left: As a widow, Olgivanna went to Tokyo to try and save Wright's Imperial Hotel from demolition in 1967.

1939

LLOYD LEWIS HOUSE

Address: 153 Little St. Mary's Road,
Libertyville, Illinois
Built: 1939

This is another of Wright's masterpiece "homes in nature," designed just prior to World War II. A shockingly modern house in every sense of the word, it was created for Lloyd Lewis, the longtime drama critic of the *Chicago Daily News*. Set within the most private of riverside estates, the house has all the erudite sophistication and edgy refinement urbane people of taste thirsted for at the close of the 1930s. Libertyville was, then, country geography some fifty miles northwest of Chicago; a place where old-money families kept vintage estates out of the public eye. Privacy was a gilded virtue here, highly prized. Along the twisting contours of the Des Plaines River, the same waterway that flows by the Coonley Estate, far to the south, Wright fashioned one of his most distinctive and defining dwellings in a new expression. With the Lloyd Lewis House, Wright engaged the prairie in a new architectural relationship. Two elements immediately seize the eye upon first seeing this woodland hideaway: its elaborate, fragrant horizontal cypress massing and its superior transitional modern form with vertical lift from its common brick foundation piers. Here is a further development of Wright's Usonian concept, particularly the intricate geometric block patterns cut into the cypress. Many consider this the first of his in-line Usonian homes. Cantilevered eaves project with a minimalist artistry, with square openings for extra light. The house is essentially two wings, the first lifted high from the riverbank by powerful brick supports containing public entryways and covered lower-level loggias.

Public rooms—the living room, dining room, and balcony—are lifted to the level of a second story, reminiscent of some of the great Prairie homes designed for the Thomases, the Coonleys, and the Tomeks. A powerfully horizontal wing, half a floor lower, projects from the main central core. It contains the private rooms of family life. Two large

Right: Wright's Lloyd Lewis House is a modern estate set in a lush woodland along the banks of the Des Plaines River. It marks the return of the architect to expansive designs of extraordinary sophistication and fresh aesthetics in what stands as his first in-line Usonian house.

bedrooms and two baths make up the interior of this cypress-clad, flat-roofed extension. Bright red piping stretched with copper-mesh screens cover the exterior façade of this bedroom wing, a practicality made necessity by the house's deep setting within nature. The Des Plaines River often overflows its banks, so the lifting of family living space above the flood plain is a serious consideration that Wright incorporated in this most modern of domestic designs. This is an aircraft carrier of a house, a tabletop dolmen of design, a woodland monastery rich in details, and almost a nod to LeCorbusier. Lloyd Lewis was a citified farmer, which led to one of Wright's rarest of all dwellings—the chicken coop that stands some fifty feet away from the house.

Above: The profile of the Lloyd Lewis private wing includes a long veranda with copper-mesh screening anchored to pipes in Wright's favorite color, bright red.

Top: Projecting open eaves of the Lloyd Lewis House allow the maximum of natural light to fill the riverside dwelling.

Above: A projecting, cantilevered roof enhances the horizontal character of the house whose main section is fashioned from common brick.

Right: A side view of the Lloyd Lewis House with Wright's carport, a modern automobile shelter that became a standard of Usonian design and later an indelible part of the larger American landscape in the 1950s.

FRANK LLOYD WRIGHT'S LIFE 1920–1939

No new buildings by Frank Lloyd Wright were designed in the surrounding Chicago area between 1915 and 1939. A period of personal and professional exile took Wright to many areas of the nation. But Chicago, Oak Park, River Forest, and the suburban communities made famous by his work were devoid of commissions during this time. The exception, however, was the 1923 rebuilding of Wright's 1895 masterpiece, the Nathan Moore House on Forest Avenue in Oak Park, following a disastrous 1922 fire. The nation moved from the wartime economy to the luxe heyday of the 1920s, only to see the economic collapse of 1929. The ensuing Depression altered the financial lives of millions of Americans. Wright returned from Japan and expanded the facility at Taliesin. Commissions, however, were slow in coming. In the early 1920s, what commissions did come to Wright were in California, among them Aline Barnsdale's Hollyhock Spring House—Residence A, its studio, and Residence B (1920)—in Hollywood. The house was heavily influenced by Mayan architecture, a new paradigm of evocative native artistry that deeply impacted Wright's personal aesthetics. In addition, Wright also designed a residence for his old friend Alice Millard, for whom he had designed a house in Highland Park, Illinois, in 1906. In the sunny climate of developing Pasadena, he built "La Miniatura" for her in 1923, a house fashioned in his new textile-block method of cast concrete. Wright would later call this his first Usonian house, a reference to a future design mode he would refine in the 1940s and 1950s—simplified, open interiors with distinct modular utility.

Wright's personal life was never easy. Catherine Tobin Wright eventually relented and gave her husband a divorce. His inability to make good choices in a romantic partner was compounded by his friendship with the sensual woman who would become his second wife, Miriam Noel. She accompanied Wright to Japan when he left to build the Imperial Hotel. She was his nurse when he became ill in Tokyo and the object of his mother's ire when she arrived to discover them together. His eventual marriage to the wealthy Noel proved a catastrophe. It would take him years to free himself from her grasp as she spiraled into mental illness. During their tempestuous marriage, Wright took up with a young aristocrat, a Yugoslavian dancer known as Olgivanna. By 1924, they were lovers and about to set off on Wright's most dangerous love affair to date. While Olgivanna divorced her husband with dispatch, Wright was in a much more difficult position with Miriam Noel Wright, who refused to divorce him. When Olgivanna discovered she was pregnant with Wright's child, she and the architect fled, taking her child by her first husband with them. A manhunt ensued, ending in Wright's eventual arrest under the Man Act. Only through the concerted efforts of Wright's few remaining influential Oak Park friends did the situation end with

Right: Miriam Noel, Wright's estranged second wife, shown here in 1925. Wright left her and went into hiding with Olgivanna, who had his child. After a bitter divorce from Miriam Noel, he later married Olgivanna and remained with her for the rest of his life.

Above: The living room of Aline Barnsdall's Hollyhock House, named for its ornamental forms. The house has been designated by the American Institute of Architects as one of the seventeen buildings designed by Wright to be retained as an example of his architectural contribution to American culture.

Wright's release from jail. Miriam Noel Wright only consented to a divorce in August of 1927. Wright and Olgivanna were immediately married.

Engaged in designs for clients with connections to the early days, Wright became involved in 1927 with the Arizona Biltmore Hotel project with Edward C. Waller Jr., the son of his early River Forest benefactor. He also fashioned a house that same year in Derby, New York, for Darwin D. Martin, brother of William E. Martin of Oak Park. The brothers were the catalysts for nearly a dozen structures by Wright among their family, friends, and business associates.

The Fellowship at Taliesin, as the compound of architectural apprentices came to be called, was further expanded with the addition of Taliesin III, in 1925, and a larger complex in 1932. Between 1928 and 1935, Wright had only six projects, of which only two were independent commissions. But when they did begin to come again in 1935, they were imbued with the deepest of the architect's organic aesthetic. At Bear Run, Pennsylvania, department-store mogul Edgar Kauffman commissioned Wright to design what ultimately became his most famous domestic dwelling, Fallingwater. With titanic, cantilevered projections lifted high above the rock and running water of a stream, Wright created an architectural wonder centered in the very heart of nature.

On the heels of Fallingwater came the commission for the Johnson Wax Administration Building in Racine, Wisconsin, a quixotic, streamlined piece of industrial marvel. This was followed by the Herbert Jacobs House in Madison, Wisconsin, the architect's first acknowledged Usonian-designed structure, and Wingspread, a luxurious dwelling in Wind Point, Wisconsin, created for Herbert Johnson of Johnson Wax in 1937, a design Wright called the last Prairie house.

In 1939, on the eve of another international conflict, Wright designed his first house back in the familiar region of Chicago: the Lloyd Lewis House in Libertyville, Illinois, along the banks of the Des Plaines River. It is a house of unique modernity and edgy Usonian aesthetics. Wright had discovered a new and final architectural design that he would spend the rest of his life perfecting into what he called "the house that democracy built."

1950

JOHN O. CARR HOUSE

Address: 1544 Portage Run, Glenview, Illinois
Built: 1950

Morning sun is profound and profuse here in the John O. Carr House, set in an unusual wooded area of suburban Glenview. Traditionally, this area was a remote country extension of the unincorporated village, sitting in the middle of woodland and greenwood. The Carr House marks an important turning point for Wright, with his return to design work in the Chicago area. No Wright structure had been built in the Chicago area since 1917. In that almost thirty-five-year period, the world had changed dramatically. So too had the world of domestic architecture. Wright's return was marked by one of his most edgy new Usonian designs, so called by the architect for his determination to refashion modern home design in the postwar world. The ultramodern, T-plan house is long and lean, set into the earth at a remarkably asymmetrical angle, streamlined to nature and absorbed by its nearness. This Usonian residence glides into the earth, reflects its order, and reverences its character. This dwelling is not in competition with nature, nor is it set to contain it. Instead, Wright fashioned a house that is one with the flow of nature, a concept that he fine-tuned in his original Prairie designs half a century earlier. At this time, in his fresh, linear simplicity, he espoused a new imperative for domestic design. The house is fashioned of Chicago common brick and cypress with copper end-flashing along the low, sloping roofline. Wright refused to remove an original oak tree in the path of the long wing that forms the T. Instead, he cut a square hole in the sloping roof through which the tree could grow. It continues

Left: This massive oak is literally growing through Wright's sleek Usonian-designed Carr House. Wright refused to let the tree be cut down when the house was being built. Instead, he accommodated its presence by cutting an opening in the wide overhang. Through the years the opening has been expanded, making room for the growing girth of the oak.

Right top: Wright's original long horizontal line of French doors is open to views of an expanding, lush nature reserve, providing the interior with a "close to nature" sense of intimacy.

Right: This addition to the Carr House has won architectural awards for its faithfulness to Wright's aesthetics.

to thrive and periodically the opening is enlarged to permit more space for the tree. The house is decoratively exotic with window portholes in the Arts and Craft style of pierced block windows. Walter Norman did the original millwork for Wright. The present owner, a distinguished architect, purchased the house from the Carr family, who only lived in the house a short time. The original house was 1,950 square feet. Following a considerable expansion of several of the rooms, the house today is 3,200 square feet, more than double its original size. The present owner noted that Wright himself felt that there was "always room to expand." The restoration was a painstaking process, taking into account Wright's most exact details, particularly in regard to the concrete masonry. It has proved to be award-winning work. The interior is richly textured with brick and Philippine mahogany. Wright's built-in furniture remains. Customized concrete masonry abounds. The kitchen is the original Wright galley design with an unusual customized refrigerator and stove. Interior glass—seventeen long, rectangular panes and French doors in the living room alone—provide an intimate view of surrounding nature. Wright included a swimming pool in the original design for the Carr family. The interior side of the T opens out to the more private side of the house, away from the entry drive. The stylized gable roof adds angularity and a refined modernist beauty. This Usonian treasure is free of clutter and external embellishment. It is a peaceful retreat set into the very heart of nature, the harbinger of a fresh style of American design.

Far left: The interior entry hall of Wright's Carr House receives expansive natural light from skylights.

Left: This interior passageway leads to a private wing containing family bedrooms and is fashioned of horizontal Philippine mahogany. The outside wall is of common brick.

Right: The living room of the Carr House includes Wright's essential hearth as a focal point, as well as built-in furniture. On the wall above the hearth are the wooden block templates used to fashion the window portholes.

ROBERT MUIRHEAD FARMHOUSE

Address: Rohrsen Road, Plato Center, Illinois
Built: 1950

It would be hard to imagine any house by Wright having a deeper bond with the Illinois prairie than the Muirhead Farmhouse, the architect's only design for a working farm. The Muirhead family has owned this farmland since 1860, some seventy-five miles due west of Chicago, near the town of Elgin, in true, rural "Land of Lincoln." Robert Muirhead received a degree in engineering from the University of Wisconsin, Madison, Wright's brief alma mater. While he returned to the family farm following graduation, he always stayed well-read in the fields of engineering and architecture. Many years later, after he had taken over the operation of the farm, while traveling to the family's Wisconsin vacation house, he pulled the family car into Taliesin, where, through a series of providential events, he met Frank Lloyd Wright. It was then that he proposed to Wright the idea of commissioning an active farmhouse. Wright was delighted by the prospect; he came to see Plato Center and was often present during the construction, well into his eighties. The result was this amazing Usonian masterpiece.

Robert Muirhead's son, Robert Jr., was a teenager when the project began and recalls numerous occasions when he would look up to see Mr. Wright's red Lincoln pulling up the entrance road. He still recalls his diminutive stature, bow ties, and vests. Even today, he still remembers that his family knew the architect was a man ahead of his time. The house has a remarkable monastic character to it—simple, austere, and demonstrably utilitarian. It is a most unusual farmhouse, fashioned of Chicago common brick from Wright's favorite, the Kerry Brickyard. All the bricks came from the same batch, which imbued them with a remarkable uniformity. Because this is a working farm, the design kept certain realities of farm life an intimate part of the structure's plan. For instance, the kitchen and dining area are located at the public end of the structure, so that farmhands could have access to meals at certain times without entering the private family wing, located down a long thirty-foot corridor. The farmhouse kitchen, a full story and a half, may be Wright's most expansive. The family wing and the public wing connect to the great cube that is the center of house life: Wright's great room, a soaring story-and-a-half room of true aesthetically minimalist proportions, is anchored by a voluminous hearth. A built-in sofa by Wright stretches the full length of the room. Floor-to-ceiling glass panes provide sweeping views of the exterior farmland setting. Throughout the house, at many corners, glass panes are set at right angles to each other in a familiar Wright extravagance. Five cypress-paneled bedrooms are almost Scandinavian in their utility and sense of

Left: The exterior of the Muirhead Farmhouse is fashioned of cypress boards and Chicago common brick. It sits low to the ground with an extended horizontal design.

proportioned order. Every nail in the paneling is countersunk and covered in beeswax. Every hinge on every door and cabinet, throughout, is a piano hinge—an intricate, tightly grooved metal fitting that more securely and stealthily fastens doors within a jamb. The master bedroom has its own large brick hearth, as does the dining room. Floors have radiant pipe heat underneath the cement surface. Muirhead children still recall the constant reminders they received as children never to set boxes of chocolate on the floor. The interiors are bright and open, reflecting the maximum of available natural light. Wright's long, horizontal design plan was revolutionary on an American farm. To many it might resemble the ubiquitous ranch house that was so popular in the 1950s and 1960s. Few ranch-style designs, however, begat the interior quality and craftsmanship as Wright designs portray. After fifty years, the Muirhead Farmhouse is about to undergo a massive restoration. A new roof, heating system, and thermal cooling system are among some of the projects anticipated. This ambitious plan will bring the house back to its original Wright design. Most of the farmland, some 800 acres, has recently been sold to the State of Illinois, which will return the land to its original prairie grass. The house itself and ten acres around it will remain in the family. Wright demonstrated the utility and inventiveness of his refined concept of an edgy domestic dwelling. This is also a relatively hidden Wright treasure; its interior is shown for the first time here.

Left: Like most Usonian designs, Wright raised the height in the kitchen to allow sufficient room for cooking fumes and steam. In the Muirhead Farmhouse, he enlarged the ceiling to a story and a half.

Above right: The Muirhead Farmhouse has an extraordinary Usonian pedigree as Wright's only structure designed for a genuine working farm. The property has been owned by the Muirhead family since 1860.

Right: The interior gallery and the great room of the Muirhead Farmhouse. An expansive hearth of Chicago common brick anchors the room that features a long built-in sofa running the width of the one-and-a-half story room.

1951

CHARLES F. GLORE HOUSE

Address: 170 Mayflower Avenue, Lake Forest, Illinois
Built: 1951

Lake Forest is the prized terrain of long-gilded pedigrees and trust funds from some of Chicago's most recognized family names. Stretching along the waters of Lake Michigan, this was originally the site of the country estates for the McCormicks, Armours, Fields, Swifts, Palmers, and other Chicago industrial and mercantile princes. The neighborhood is thick with baronial homes designed by America's most noted architects, such as Howard Van Doren Shaw, David Adler, Charles Frost, and Henry Ives Cobb. In the midst of all the refined, revivalist architecture, Wright designed a true 1950s modern house that in many ways was the apotheosis of his American style. Sleek, angular, practical, and unembellished in many ways, it is much like his other Usonian designs. But here in Lake Forest, where grandeur is aplenty, Wright gave the Glores a splendid modern mansion replete with a two-story living room that makes this house unique. The soaring, two-story angular window glass rises like a cathedral beneath the sweeping, gabled roof whose eaves are deep and remarkably sheltering. The roof's dramatic cantilevering has its roots in the noble traditions of structures like the Mrs. Thomas Gale House of half a century prior. The exterior walls of the Glore House are of pink Chicago common brick, presumably from Kelly's Brickyard, Wright's favorite Chicago manufacturer. Built overlooking a dramatic ravine on almost two acres of land that is edged into nature, the Glore House is expressive of the architect's ultimate concept of organic design, his belief that architecture must arise out of nature itself. Though the structure appears small for a Usonian dwelling, it has five bedrooms, four and a half baths, and four fireplaces, large by Wright's standards. Interior walls are of exposed brick with handsome Honduran mahogany widely used throughout. Wright incorporated some highly practical built-in features: particularly noteworthy is the dining room table and seating arrangement placed in a separate room, unusual in a utilitarian Usonian design. The architect also repeated the long gallery that he introduced in the Muirhead Farmhouse as a means of spacing the private "quiet" rooms from the more public areas. Wright's use of glass is an important feature of the overall plan of the house. It makes the grandeur of nature at one with the activity of the dwelling, within easy reach aesthetically. It is a remarkable change from the small, high windows in many Prairie dwellings that permitted only framed portraits of the outside. The Glore House has been well cared for through the last half century and remains a stunning expression of Usonian design.

Previous page: The two-story, pink-brick, Usonian-designed Glore House appears to have the capacity for flight with its spacious winglike span of a roof. Its sleek, trim modernity projects a sense of uncluttered utility, the hallmark of Wright's final architectural style.

Right: An aerial view of the Glore House demonstrates Wright's modern passion for long, narrow, expansive design that is compact and practical, yet elegant and sophisticated.

1954

LOUIS B. FREDERICK HOUSE

Address: 28 West 248 County Line Road,
Barrington Hills, Illinois
Built: 1954

For Wright the concept of the Usonian house was not only architectural, it was a philosophical construct as well. It evolved toward the end of the 1930s as his deepening awareness of the need to create domestic architecture that was further supportive of family living became an imperative that he had already attempted to resolve in his Prairie designs, but that still needed to become more utilitarian, more affordable, and, at the same time, more innovative. He knew that there was a larger client base than those with the deep pockets of his early commissions. Usonian design stripped away needless embellishment and excess that drove up price. It also showed the bigger fact that social conditions were themselves changing in America. Prairie-designed homes in the late Edwardian era before World War I always made provisions for household staff. Most American families lived without that luxury. Usonian design was about a new form of American domestic dwelling.

The catalyst for Wright's commission from Louis B. Frederick was the client's discovery of the Usonian model house at an exhibition staged on the future site of the Guggenheim Museum on Fifth Avenue in New York. This led to the Fredericks meeting with Wright in a Chicago hotel and their agreement on the appropriateness of a Usonian house for the refined wooded terrain of Barrington Hills—Chicago's most aristocratic region. The most modern of Wright's designs was ideal for Frederick, an executive with the refined Chicago furniture and interior-design firm of Colby's. The result was a superb 3,300-square-foot house of Roman brick and wood set on a hill, part of an eleven-acre site surrounded by oaks and hawthorns. The gabled roof introduced a rich angularity.

Three bedrooms, two baths, and a spacious family room with a massive triangular fireplace are wrapped in Philippine mahogany, a favorite interior wood of Wright's. Vaulted ceilings and clerestory windows provide both interior depth and intense natural light. The floors are concrete with a radiant heating system built in, similar to what Wright did at the Muirhead Farmhouse a few years earlier. The placement of a playroom, which doubled as a guest room, down a thirty-foot-long gallery is also very similar to the design Wright employed at the Muirhead farm. It is said that some 50,000 Cranbrook buckskin-hued bricks were used in the construction of this country house. Wright's use of these narrow pressed bricks is reminiscent of his similar use of them in the Heurtley House in Oak Park.

ALLEN FRIEDMAN HOUSE

Address: 200 Thornapple,
Bannockburn, Illinois
Built: 1956

The Allen Friedman House has the distinction of being the last house of Frank Lloyd Wright's to be built during his lifetime. It was under construction in the final days of his life in 1959. Allen Friedman was Wright's client and a man of vision who had become enamored with the architect's dramatic modernity expressed in the stark linear simplicity of the Usonian style. For all its understated utilitarianism, this house has an amazing grasp of the Illinois prairie that many of Wright's more robust Prairie-style residences never attained.

Originally built on a generous five-acre parcel of land just south of Lake Forest, the house today is still in touch with the tall grass and prairie plantings that surround this uniquely shaped dwelling that is very much a skipjack of the flat land, a reminder of those shallow-bottomed American boats of the nineteenth century. Because of the house's low profile, it appears to dwell upon the horizon. Two wings sit at curious angles to the earth, one set at 120 degrees, the other at sixty degrees, dramatizing the horizontal sweep of the house. The anchor of the structure is the chimney, always an important feature of every Wright house, but here the chimney itself is a major part of the house, not just a rooftop appendage. Its cubic massing is the very axis of the home, architecturally and emotionally. On the interior, the ten-foot hearth is the center of family living in this 3,500-square-foot house.

The low-rising exterior has a sweeping horizontal character fashioned of terra cotta–colored common brick. The horizontal line is further extended by the narrow banding of geometric windows of block-shaped glass that stretches across the upper level of the outside wall. The low, hipped roof is embellished with elaborate decorative copper banding along the roof edge. This stylized pattern continues along the edge of the loggia roof that connects with the garage angled from the main entryway. Deep-set eaves are a familiar Wright design feature. On the private, interior side of the house a spacious lawn rolls to the green wood, a scene

Above: View of the Allen Friedman House entryway, a solid mass of ruby port common brick that reaches giant proportion in the cubical chimney housing an interior ten-foot hearth. A long, sweeping, modern loggia with exterior copper ornamentation covers the walkway to the carport, an essential element of any Usonian design.

Above: The anterior side of the Friedman House displays its low-rising, demonstrable horizontal Usonian form, a shape made unique by the curious angle of the home's two sleek wings of 120 degrees and sixty degrees.

Left: The portholes have an Arts and Crafts origin and are utilized beneath the roof flashing. Weathered copper runs the length of the roof edge.

that engulfs the house and serves as the prime panorama of the prairie seen from inside the house. The interior of the house is filled with many original Wright features, from the kitchen skylight that is a prominent ventilation feature in Usonian design to the heavy-duty midcentury appliances and counters in the kitchen, the built-in hardwood dining room table, and the long, built-in sofa-bench lining a wall of the living room. The present residents are only the second owners, having purchased the house from the Friedmans. They have a deep sense of artistic reverence for this last Wright Usonian project that the Taliesin Association saw through to completion following Wright's death. Interior rooms are wide and flowing, rich in Philippine mahogany. Wright sought a new American harmony in this design that is easily seen in the peacefulness and quiet of this simple dwelling.

FRANK LLOYD WRIGHT'S LIFE 1940–1949

During the 1940s, Wright had a boom period of work with some sixty-two designs that, when completed, stretched from Lakeland, Florida, to Pleasantville, New York, and from Carmel and Malibu, California, to Kalamazoo, Michigan, and Quasqueton, Iowa. Such an expansive geography demonstrates Wright's remarkable ability for self-invention and professional resiliency. He began the decade at seventy-three years of age, still vibrant, eccentric, argumentative, and potentially dangerous. Wright would spend the war years as a staunch pacifist, going so far as to secure conscientious objector status for many of his Taliesin apprentices. Coupled with his years of work in Japan and his affection for the Japanese culture, he was the object of frequent investigation by J. Edgar Hoover and the FBI, a shadow that would dog him for the remainder of his life.

The period was rich in Wright's new, evolving Usonian designs that, even more than his Prairie style, seemed to be shaping a streamlined, utilitarian modernity, not only of architectural design, but also of lifestyle for the client who chose one. Wright appeared to be applying a totally new standard of efficiency to his new model of domestic dwelling. The uncluttered surprise contained in the Usonian concept was deeply American, the kind of spunky, energized, utopian spirit that the United States was engaging in at the time.

Wright's Usonian homes were simple and all about function. Taking their cue from what Wright had discovered in the homes of the Japanese, they were usually single-story structures, open and flowing with the natural movement of human beings in the process of their lives. Bedrooms occupied the same spatial plane as the public rooms of family function, though removed to a separate wing for privacy and quiet. Wright renamed the kitchen the "workspace," and made it compact, efficient, and technologically sophisticated. The usual division of rooms became a thing of the past, with the dining area and social area connected as one. Often, the houses were set into the earth with the wings at dramatic angles to one another. His introduction of a cover space for the family car, called the carport, remains a lasting contribution of Wright's to the larger cultural language of suburban America.

Usonian was more than just a type of house, it was a way of looking at the world and one's life. The bric-a-brac and ornamentation of the past were jettisoned by the crisp practicality of a house made for the modern age. Wright struggled to make such homes affordable to the general public, as during the 1940s they still carried a high price tag. Usonian homes of this period had a special relationship to the land on which they were built—often large properties in prestigious locations with celebrated mountain views or secluded woodland glades. Postwar

Right: The Herbert Jacobs House is considered to be the first Usonian house. It was designed in an L-plan.

production growth in available building materials invigorated the housing market that had slowed to a trickle. Among his most stunning projects was the Walter Residence in Quasqueton, Iowa, built along the bluffs of the Wapsipinicon River, completed in 1948, with a 900-square-foot living room, a huge outdoor hearth, a river pavilion, and the regulation carport.

Wright also designed a Unitarian church in 1947 in Shorewood, Wisconsin, which counted among their earliest members, in the previous century, the architect's

own parents. Its soaring, angular copper roof has the aesthetics of a stripped-down space-age cathedral. With expansive glass, common brick, and cypress trim, Wright reinvented the American home through his exhaustive refinement of the Usonian-plan design.

Below: The Herbert Jacobs House was built of brick and redwood—materials that were to become typical of future Usonian houses.

1957

DONALD DUNCAN HOUSE, MARSHALL ERDMAN PREFABRICATED HOMES

Address: 2255 Edgebrook Drive, Lisle, Illinois
Built: 1957

Wright's abiding drive to create architecture that was emblematic of American democracy was an evolving art. From Prairie to Usonian, Wright sought architecture that was, at its heart, economical, as well as structurally significant. At the dawn of World War I, his American Systems-Built homes designed for Arthur J. Richards attempted to cement that ideal. In the 1950s, he furthered that long dream by his designs for the Marshall Erdman Company with his prefabricated homes. Unlike the process of labor-intensive fabrication that was so much a part of most Wright designs, Erdman was able to precut and partially assemble many sections of these structures before they were shipped to the building site. Construction was simplified, thus reducing costs. Three distinct designs were created by Wright, though only two of the three were ever built.

The Duncan Home in the far-western Chicago suburb of Lisle is an example of Wright's Prefab #1 design. Nine of this particular model were built. Donald and Elizabeth Duncan discovered this user-friendly design of Wright's in a 1956 feature on the Erdman prefabricated designs in *House & Home* magazine. Like many other clients of Wright's, Donald Duncan was an electrical engineer, the familiar blend of inventive character and practical thinker so common among those intrigued by the architect. The couple had always been under the belief that Wright's work was meant for the wealthy. The article, however, sold them on the practicality and economy of the Erdman Prefab. The Duncans met with Marshall Erdman directly about the purchase and construction of their home, for which they paid $47,000 at the time. It was not an inexpensive house. In true Usonian fashion, the three-bedroom house rose low to the ground, with a gabled roof sloping deeply along the front. A solid masonry cube is the core of the house with a long, low wing projecting from it. It is standard in each of these homes. Concrete block is used for the cube here in the Duncan House. This geometric cube connects to a remarkably long, horizontal rectangle, the wing that provides the house with its sleek, angular modern style.

Though the exterior is reminiscent of Wright's popular and familiar board-and-batten cladding, the skin is actually painted panels of Masonite siding with added decorative horizontal battens. Windows are wide and narrow, set in pairs along the front, rising up to the deep overhang, deepening the horizontal line. The basic plan

Above: The profile of the Duncan House has a great flowing horizontal character projecting from the main masonry cube on the left through the sleek extending wing.

of the house is the familiar in-line plan with slight variation. One way in which Wright was able to ensure cost cutting was by permitting the use of standard doors and windows made by American manufacturers. His willingness to dispense with the costly custom-made hardware of past designs helped to keep costs down. Wright made innovation a regular feature of his design, introducing economical forced-air heating in this new model home, an improvement over his previous work thanks to the growing technological advances of the postwar period. Bedrooms were arranged along the quiet side of the house, keeping with Wright's preference for separating noisy public space from the more private side of family space. Rising construction costs ultimately made the Erdman Prefab not as economical as many hoped.

Tragically, after nearly fifty years, development within the suburb of Lisle has threatened the Duncan House with possible demolition. Wright's defenders are cautious and watchful over this innovative design that was a synthesis of the architect's struggle to make housing that was both architectural and affordable.

CARL POST HOUSE, MARSHALL ERDMAN PREFABRICATED HOMES

Address: 265 Donlea Road,
Barrington Hills, Illinois
Built: 1957

Developer Al Borah built this Usonian residence, a Marshall Erdman Prefabricated Home, in the far northwest Chicago suburb of Barrington Hills. In the 1950s, Barrington Hills was hardly what might be described as a typical suburban community. Located in the heart of hunting country, this was a place where old money kept rambling country houses on great acreages of land behind large fences and hedgerows. Homes here must be built on no less than five acres. Barrington Hills' quiet refinement has an air of gentility and remote elegance. The wooded terrain and verdant landscape were still wild in the 1950s, with homes tucked away down long frontage drives that covered the hearty homes hidden from public view by ivy-covered walls.

Pristine nature was always a well-chosen site for any Wright design, even one that has been prefabricated for the sake of economical construction. The architect himself would have highly approved of Barrington Hills as a place well suited for a Wright dwelling. Borah showed an intense sense of an appropriate setting in constructing this most modern of houses in the rich countryside of Illinois. Almost as soon as the house was completed, he had a buyer, Carl Post.

So significant was the entire project of its construction and the sparkling Wright pedigree that went along with its high inventiveness that the National Association of Home Builders had tours of the site during their annual convention in Chicago in January 1958. Slight variations in the materials used on the house differentiate it from other similar models. Whereas the Duncan House used concrete block for its masonry core, the Post House used the more expensive brick design.

Right: On the left, the square masonry cube containing public rooms can be seen. Extending from this is the lower, more horizontal wing containing private family rooms, an essential element of this prefab design.

Above: The interior of the Post House is warmed by the expansive use of wood throughout the long gallery that links the public areas with the more private bedroom wing.

Left: The interior of the Carl Post House demonstrates the high rise in the slanted ceiling and the infusion of natural light that were important design features for Wright.

The house also has one more bedroom than the standard three-bedroom model of the Duncan House. In addition, the twelve-foot-wide master bedroom here is also generously expanded. The basic imprint, however, is the same—gabled roof and Masonite panel siding with decorative horizontal batten stripping that accentuate the horizontal character of the house. The interior is open and spacious, with additional brickwork used in the central hearth. Other expansions, such as the breezeway between the garage and the kitchen, further enlarge the standard design, demonstrating the versatility of Wright's design and the elasticity of the prefabrication. Seven other houses in the Prefab #1 style were built in addition to the Post and Duncan houses, four in Wisconsin, two in New York, and one in Minnesota. Only two homes in the Prefab #2 style, essentially a great one-room dwelling, were ever built, one in Wisconsin and the other in Minnesota. They remain symbols of the midcentury modern age in which utility, economy, and modernity fashioned a home that was affordable and low maintenance. It was a combination that was not quite ever able to be achieved, bringing to a close Wright's last great innovation in American domestic design.

FRANK LLOYD WRIGHT'S LIFE 1950–1959

There is a cool irony that the last decade of Wright's life as an architect should be as exciting and provocative as his first, when designs came fast and always caused talk. It has been said that when Wright would draw a design, the only thing left to do was place the furniture and move in, so thorough were the details of his designs. It never let up, even when he reached the age of eighty-three in 1950. His marriage to Olgivanna was in its twenty-third year. Many of the estrangements of the past were renegotiated. A chance meeting with Frederick C. Robie Jr. at the Sherman House Hotel in Chicago revived some of the early triumphs of more than fifty years before. The 1950s would bring Wright enormous celebrity. He was not the only member of the family to be part of popular culture. His granddaughter, the Hollywood actress Anne Baxter, would achieve her own fame.

Wright was a great link in American culture. His colorful demeanor was made for television and the emerging technologies of the cold war. America was expanding across the continental landscape, reshaping livable space, and inventing new suburbs from coast to coast. Nothing was more valuable than a new home, especially one that arose out of the passionate necessity caused by the postwar baby boom.

Wright produced some 121 designs during the 1950s, a number he had not equaled since the first decade of the twentieth century. Remarkably, seven of those homes were in the Chicago area and represent some of his most vital work. Each structure stands with remarkable strength and power as some of the brightest

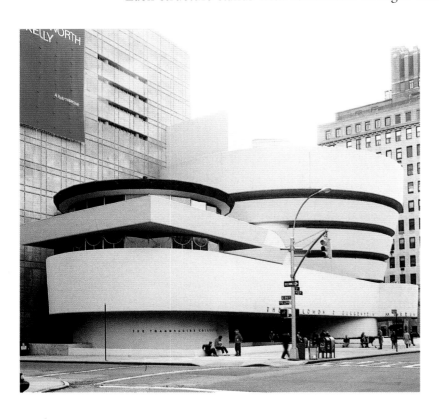

architectural achievements in American history. These Usonian dwellings make a fantastic use of nature through their simple, yet dramatic, utilitarian design, beginning with the 1950 design of the John O. Carr House in Glenview, Illinois, that marked Wright's return to the Chicago region where he had his gilded start. That same year, he took on one of his most evocative commissions from Robert Muirhead, a prairie farmer in Kane County, Illinois, for whom Wright designed the only working farmhouse of his entire career. It was a project

Above and inset: The Guggenheim Museum is built around an ascending spiral ramp. It is notable for the inventive use of concrete and its bold geometric form.

Left: The Guggenheim opened to the public in 1959, six months after Wright died. The museum acts as a reminder of the architect's creative originality and ability to shock.

that brought Wright back to the very beginnings of his architectural aesthetic—the flat, windswept Illinois prairie that had unleashed spirit and inspiration into everything to which Wright set his hand. The theory, praxis, and synthesis of his career, his Taliesin dream, and his euphoric sense of American utopianism merged in the shining glory of the Muirhead Farmhouse. In some of Chicago's most aristocratic country locales—Lake Forest and Barrington Hills—Wright achieved masterful designs for a succession of Usonian houses of delicate, organic expression and harmonious engagement of the surrounding extraordinary natural environment.

By the middle of the decade, the architect had fashioned the last component of his lifelong dream of affordable housing of significant architectural design—the Marshall Erdman Prefabricated Home. Wright stripped away all the excess elements that traditionally raised the cost of his designs. What he provided was substantive architectural design for materials that could be assembled offsite. Later these pieces and components could be assembled at the construction site, saving both time and money. In addition, Wright permitted doors and windows to be fabricated by ordinary American manufacturers, foregoing the very expensive, hand-wrought, one-of-a-kind items that made his designs so expensive. The architect was ninety years old when he and Marshall Erdman put forth what he saw as essentially an emblem of American democracy—the well-made, economically affordable home. Two such structures were built in the Chicago area.

Perhaps the most remarkable design of Frank Lloyd Wright from this era is the building with which he is most identified—the Solomon R. Guggenheim Museum on Fifth Avenue in New York City. Its confounding modern swirl and bold geometric character is today as much a part of the profile of Manhattan as the Chrysler Building or Rockefeller Center. It is appropriate that his final design should be something so dramatic and public in nature. At the center of the world's most significant geography, Wright left an eternal legacy in sleek, streamlined concrete, the material with which he fashioned his Unity Temple more than half a century before.

Frank Lloyd Wright died in Phoenix, Arizona, on April 9, 1959, just months before his ninety-second birthday. He had been hospitalized shortly before the end, while visiting his beloved Taliesin West in the Arizona desert. Today, his remains have been mingled with those of his dearest Olgivanna, the woman with whom he did find some happiness and peace. They are buried beneath the desert clay at Taliesin West. He was not an easy man to know or engage in common effort. But, he was a man of invention and artistry with the gift of a singular American vision that transformed the landscape of the nation and the manner in which many of its people lived. He provided the nation with its most endemic architectural expression in the era of its most inventive and expansive coming-of-age.

COUNTRY RETREATS NEAR CHICAGO

Frank Lloyd Wright designed a number of lake houses for wealthy clients within easy reach of Chicago, in the areas of Ogden Dunes, Lake Delavan, and Grand Beach. Although these houses were not in the city itself, they were built for Chicagoans who wanted a place nearby to escape from the bustle of the city. These areas have long been favorites of Chicago residents seeking country retreats.

ANDREW F. ARMSTRONG HOUSE, OGDEN DUNES

Address: 43 Cedar Trail, Ogden Dunes, Indiana
Built: 1939

The Ogden Dunes is, today, a national park. Less than forty-five minutes from downtown Chicago, the sandy geography of Lake Michigan's southern underbelly is a strange combination of majestic natural wonder and brawny steel-mill industrial might. Amid the birches and pines here, Wright built one of his most elegant dwellings, carved in, seemingly, to the nature that enfolds it. The Armstrong House, as the structure is known, was named for its first owner, Andrew F. H. Armstrong, who lived in the house for the first nineteen years. The present owner and his family have lived here for the past forty-five years. During this period, the house has been meticulously maintained and restored with painstaking accuracy.

Of all the Wright houses in the Chicago region, no house occupies its place in nature with more streamlined grandeur. The house has a unique character that is first and foremost the product of its remarkable vertical elevation. That sweep is extended further by the horizontal massing of its six different flat-roofed levels. The angles of the roof are unique. The lower portions of the structure fashion a far-reaching series of brick wall massings, in a deep, rich, almost wine-colored terra-cotta brick. The family room, living room, dining room, and kitchen are on the lower level of the house. Bedrooms are located in a level above this, separated from the public area in much the same way as Wright designed in the Coonley House.

The interior is rich with exotic woods, mahogany and cedars, that still perfume the air. Ceilings are high in the public rooms, with expansive vistas to the lake and surrounding dunes. It is said that Frank Lloyd Wright himself sat in the living room in one of his built-in sofas and saw that the view of the lake was obscured

Right: Built into its own dune, the Armstrong House rises high out of nature, its personality fashioned from the progressive series of plateau roofs, Wright's signature seal.

ever so slightly by one of the exterior horizontal cypress boards. He ordered the offending board removed so that the full lake view was obtained. In the late 1960s, John H. Howe, an architect with prestigious links to Wright and the community at Taliesin, restored and enlarged the house for the present owner. The house doubled in size from the additions, while adhering to the ethos of the great architect at all times. Better-insulated thermal glass replaced the original panels. There is no denying the shadows of Wright's extensive Japanese influence in the linear majesty of this dwelling. Clean lines abound throughout this dramatically modern house, though it is far from Usonian, Wright's midcentury modern genre of ranch-style dwellings.

For all its grandeur, this is one of the "hidden" Wright homes, a structure with the appearance of a great, cantilevered treehouse. If ever a house displayed Wright's concept of "organic" design, it is this stunning secret masterpiece, the architect's first house built near Chicago in two decades.

Left: From its high vantage point atop its sand dune, the Armstrong House enjoys panoramas of both the woods and Lake Michigan seashore, satisfying Wright's passion for a location with an intimate proximity to nature.

Right: Deeply projecting eaves, a significant element of Wright's signature style, add enhanced character to the proportions of the Armstrong House.

LAKE DELAVAN, WISCONSIN

Lake Delavan, Wisconsin, is a convenient weekend country location less than a two-hour car ride from Chicago. Many Chicagoans have made this a favorite getaway place since the late nineteenth century. The surrounding shoreline and woodland setting are thick with small cabins, cottages, and great waterfront homes. In the last years of the nineteenth century and the start of the twentieth century, Frank Lloyd Wright designed five such masterpieces along the southern reach of the lake within a one-mile area. Their architectural significance underlines Wright's versatility in the variety of Prairie designs and adaptability to both client economy and the natural environment. These houses are fixed in the context of some of Wright's most significant works. They reflect the evolution of his Prairie design thematic, as well as providing him with the opportunity to experiment with fresh ideas more reflective of the remote Wisconsin terrain.

HENRY WALLIS (WALLIS-GOODSMITH) HOUSE AND BOATHOUSE

Address: 3407 South Shore Drive,
Lake Delavan, Wisconsin
Built: Boathouse 1897, House 1900

This is the first of Wright's Lake Delavan lake houses. Its name reflects the fact that Henry Wallis built the house and quickly sold it to Mr. Goodsmith; hence the hyphenated designation. The Wallis–Goodsmith House is perched at the top of a great rolling lawn that stretches up from the shoreline, wide and expansive. Entering the house from the main road at the back of the property brings visitors through the elaborate covered walkway beside the swimming pool. The Asian influence of this loggia is demonstrable and a reminder of the imaginative pagoda

Below: The main entrance from the driveway of the Wallis-Goodsmith House is an expansive pergola, or garden trellis, fashioned in the same sculptured board-and-batten cladding as the house. Its Asian sensibilities are later reflected in the Foster House.

house Wright designed for Judge Foster in Chicago, with which it is contemporaneous. An important unifying design feature of the Wallis-Goodsmith House is the rough-hewed, horizontal, board-and-batten cladding that begins at the rear entry and enwraps the entire lake home. Originally designed in pine, exterior wood has been replaced with cedar. Great horizontal massing is achieved by the use of this eminently successful material favored by Wright and used in countless Prairie-style dwellings.

The Wallis-Goodsmith House contains one of Wright's most dramatic entranceways, with high, projecting, contoured board-and-batten walls that shield a deep passageway that enwraps the entry stairway. On a much more expansive scale, this entry has strong similarities with the Foster House. A graceful, hipped roof extends in generous overhangs. Exterior stucco cladding stretches from the second-story sill line up

Above: The house as seen from the bottom of the long, spacious lawn leading to the lake edge. From this vantage point, Wright's spacious horizontal aesthetic is prominently displayed.

to the projection of the eaves. Horizontal wood banding adds a continuous ornamental line above the second-story windows and at the level of the sills, giving a geometric framing to the façade. Panoramas of the lake view are broad and bold across the rectangular frontage end that faces the water. A wide lawn rolls down to the water where Wright originally constructed the 1897 boathouse. It has since been demolished.

The broad sweep of land on which the house sits provides panoramic perspectives of the house. The deep overhangs, horizontal cladding, and rectangular window treatments have echoes of the Millard House in Highland Park. Each is surprisingly simple in design, but achieves effective expression through understated profiles. Multiple rooflines add to the horizontal character of the Wallis-Goodsmith House. Cladding provides the house with a unique texture that is singularly Wright. Four large, horizontally rectangular windows create a wall of glass open to the lake. Wright's lake houses are hidden gems, often outside the accessibility of Wright enthusiasts. Their locations are more private than many of Wright's better-known houses of this period in which he was developing his Prairie design. The Wallis-Goodsmith House is among his earliest works in his native state of Wisconsin.

Left: A shielded entry and tapered board-and-batten cladding are among Wright's hallmarks here. The horizontal line he created gives remarkable symmetry to this massive dwelling.

PENWERN, FRED B. JONES HOUSE (1900); GATE LODGE WITH WATER TOWER AND GREENHOUSE; BARN WITH STABLES; BOATHOUSE

Address: 3335 South Shore Drive,

Lake Delavan, Wisconsin

Built: House 1900, Water Tower, Greenhouse 1901,

Boathouse 1900 (burned 1975)

Penwern, as the Fred B. Jones House is known, may be among Wright's most elaborate and luxurious estates, in the genre of the Coonley Estate. It may also contain the most expansive interiors of a Wright dwelling, so massive and generous are its high ceilings, sweeping verandas, large bedrooms, and staircases. The main residence is distinguished by two distinct features. First is the dramatic use of multiple gabled roofs of deep angularity set high and in perfect proportion to one another throughout the house. The second is the significant extension of the porte cochere, powerfully horizontal in its projection and strongly vertical in its towering height. The great sweeping arch of the porte cochere is repeated along the lakefront façade of the house in the expansive veranda. Both are architecturally enriching geometric flourishes. The porte cochere becomes an open loggia with passage to a tower room that was once the private domain of gentlemen card players. Wright provided one of his most eccentric design features here, a hammered tin urinal in the corner of the room, added for the benefit of the card-game players at the turn of the century. The house itself is baronial, with a fresh and modern openness that flows from its sheer size. Horizontal board-and-batten rough-sawed cladding extends

Above: The grand loggia at Penwern bridges the main house to its gabled tower and serves as a dramatic porte cochere.

Right: Penwern is Wright's most elaborate estate on the Wisconsin waters of Lake Delavan. Its stately, countrified rock-clad walls and steep triple gables create an aristocratic profile.

Above: The side view of the stable of Penwern exhibits rising gables and board-and-batten cladding with horizontal banding.

throughout. Foundation walls and piers across the structure are made of handsome stone boulders that enhance the exterior with a true country patina. The interior designs and furnishings are on a scale that is nothing short of opulent for a Wright dwelling. Vast rooms, high-ceilinged and adorned with rich hardwoods, create a textured comfort far larger than any of the architect's previous designs. This large-scale proportioning continues throughout the house. The great room contains a massive Roman-brick fireplace, among the most expansive in any Wright dwelling. Its size fits the room. Another large-size hearth of narrow Roman brick is in the dining room, anchoring the grandeur of its setting that among other features includes a large built-in breakfront and rich, diamond-leaded windows. The Prairie motif here is expressive of the Arts and Crafts movement, reminiscent of Wright's own home and studio. The vaulting of the veranda and the porte cochere echo his children's vaulted

Above: The crisp, country, Prairie-style elegance of Penwern begins at the Gatehouse with its refined gabled roof.

playroom. Throughout Penwern, enlarged wood trim bands the interior throughout. An oversized staircase is wide and open and features one of the home's most elegant of woods. Other buildings across the estate are fashioned in similar board-and-batten horizontal cladding and feature more gabled roofs. The gatehouse is an elaborately expansive, horizontal two-story structure with a deep entry porte cochere and an elongated roofline. Stone, matching that used on the main house, features prominently in its exterior massing. Though Penwern is an exotic country mansion, it is one of the more comfortable Wright designs and achieves a remarkable civility without narrowing any feature of this Prairie masterpiece. First and foremost, this is a country retreat that Wright has fashioned to engage the sights and sounds of nearby nature.

CHARLES S. ROSS HOUSE

Address: 3211 South Shore Drive,
Lake Delavan, Wisconsin
Built: 1902

This is a house wrapped in lake winds and built into a sloping hill. Wright's generously proportioned "cottage," built for Chicago stockbroker Charles S. Ross is set deep into the tree-lined landscape that ends at the water's edge. This is a true Prairie house, though critics often posit that such houses are often quite far from the prairie. So rustic is this house and its nearby mates that they have come to be known as "Forest" houses, structures with the same genetic architectural code as Prairie designs, but expressive of an unusual woodland character. The Ross House is considered the finest of the Forest houses. The present owner and his family christened their lake house "Forest House" long ago. Many telltale features of Wright's Prairie synthesis are at work here. The exterior cladding is rough-sawed board-and-batten horizontal boards. Originally, the boards were stained a dark brown, giving the house an exterior connection to the River Forest Tennis Club. Today, however, the outside boards are a pale yellow and the trim is a dark green that has changed some of its original character. But the elegance and grandeur of this house still retains an Edwardian aristocracy. Hipped roofs slope in multiplaned geometric refinement. At the rear of the house, there is a stunning Prairie water tower, a totem repeating the generous overhang that adds protection and shadow to this dwelling. Originally the tower contained the washhouse, where laundry chores were taken care of by the staff. Quarters above the garage along the entry drive once provided living space for servants. Today, it accommodates the owners' grandchildren. The design plan is in familiar Prairie cruciform, with the house sitting perpendicular to the lake, making the best use of the spacious land on which it sits. There is a bold horizontal character to the structure and large stones—seen in excess at the Jones House—further enhance the country motif here. Throughout, Prairie touches abound. While many of

Right: Wright applied remarkable Prairie-style aesthetics to the design of the Charles Ross House on Lake Delavan, particularly in the water tower with its expansive, hipped roof and overhanging eaves.

Wright's original interior designs have been removed over the century, interior art glass and some built-in furniture remain rich and evocative of Wright's customizing hand. Nickel caming promotes the Prairie character throughout the windows and an interior door that was once the main entryway. A large Roman-brick fireplace centers the activities of the interior. This may be one of Wright's most comfortable and colorful interiors, though its cozy and bright setting has little of Wright within. Wright never designed these homes as year-round residences; they were never insulated for the gripping Wisconsin winters. Today, however, they can be enjoyed season after season. Along the exterior, a methodically well-organized design plan still shapes the walkways and garden paths. The addition of an exterior lighting system has been fashioned in a Prairie motif. Low board-and-batten walls hold graceful Prairie urns of cast iron. The Ross House strongly influenced another of Wright's summerhouses, the Stewart House in Montecito, California, of 1909. Along the waters of Lake Delavan, Wright showed delight in laying out a domestic residence in the very heart of nature, surrounded by the woodland and lake shore of Wisconsin from which he originated.

Far left: This was the original art-glass front door, in a Prairie motif pattern, of the Ross House that has since had its open front entry enclosed both for modern heating purposes and security.

Left: The interior of the Ross House still retains some of the original built-in furniture by Wright. Here, a handsome breakfront holds dishware and linens in the dining room.

Left: Classical, wide urns are placed strategically along the exterior of the Ross House to bring the presence of nature closer to the windows and to help frame the views with lush plants.

GEORGE W. SPENCER HOUSE

Address: 3209 South Shore Drive,
Lake Delavan, Wisconsin
Built: 1902

The George W. Spencer House sits near the Charles S. Ross House. Spencer was the son-in-law of Charles Ross, so there was, from the beginning, a sense of close-knit family about the house. They share similar lake views and rolling lawns to the water's edge. This is one of Wright's Forest houses, so called because of their craftlike patina of rough-hewn board-and-batten horizontal cladding. While the lower floor demonstrates the familiar horizontal line that is so much a part of the Prairie-style, the second story is reversed, with the cladding running vertically. Despite Wright's intention of utilizing both types of boards from the very beginning, the contrasting boards have been the occasion for another of the many myths that surround the architect. There seems little truth to the story that he only discovered the anomaly when riding by on horseback, prompting his "disowning" the house. The most dramatic design feature here is the elaborate projecting open porch with exceedingly deep overhangs on the lakeside. The overhangs are both practical and elegant, shielding porch dwellers from the unpredictability of nature. The underside of the porch roof is a ship's rigging of timbers that create a pavilion of old-fashioned charm. The projection appears as a type of bowhead and deep, sloping eaves project from the hipped roof of the second story. Framing of the first-story windows continues in a line enhancing the horizontal line. On the second story, a vertical corner banding projects from above the lower windows to the roofline. Windows along the side of the house are set in a Prairie arrangement, linear and artistic. This was the smallest of Wright's Lake Delavan cottages. A large addition, repeating the design of the house on the lakeside, has been added, greatly expanding the sheer volume of the cottage. Like other Wright country cottages, the Spencer House was not winterized and use was strictly meant for the summer months. The present owner recalls discovering old newspapers from 1928 shoved between the walls as a primitive attempt at insulation. Today, the house is fully insulated and enjoys the optimum of use year-round. The house had no bathroom in the early days. A small guesthouse had a version of a privy until it burned down. The then-owner added a full bath as a result. Like the neighboring Ross House, the Spencer House wears contemporary exterior paint, white with green trim. The house remains a rustic treasure from an era in which people built summer homes to fit the countryside in which they dwelled.

Above: **The interior beams of the veranda of the Spencer House provide the extensive projecting eaves with strength.**

Above: The George Spencer House along the waters of Lake Delavan has the curious blending of both horizontal and vertical board-and-batten plank siding. It is the next-door neighbor of the Ross House.

Above: The roof extensions of the A. P. Johnson House are expansive and create remarkable modern sight lines.

Left: The central entryway door of the A. P. Johnson House is offset to the left of the structure's center and fills the whole of the entry passage.

A. P. JOHNSON HOUSE

Address: 3455 South Shore Drive, Lake Delavan, Wisconsin

Built: 1905

Little of a lake cottage persona exudes from the A. P. Johnson House. Instead, it has the feel of a great Oak Park Prairie manse. Its size and mass are baronial; its linear character palatial. This house is set on a very large piece of property that stretches from the main road outside all the way to the water's edge. It is a classic two-story cruciform structure with graceful hipped roofs and deep overhangs. A large, low-rising central chimney anchors the axis of the dwelling. The central core of the house is a powerful two-story cube with expansive projecting single-story wings with deep cantilevering. The roofs are all extensive in their sweep. The exterior cladding is horizontal tongue-and-groove planking that resembles board-and-batten. On the backside of the house, tapering pilasters project from the façade, running up to the level of the second-story sill line. They reinforce the preshadowing of later Wright designs at the Hunt House in LaGrange and the Evans House on the South Side of Chicago. The house is richly bejeweled with some of Wright's most beautiful and simple art glass. Prairie leading defines its pedigree. Windows band the upper area of the second story. Across the first floor, tall windows span the lakeside, providing dramatic panoramas. This is a large residence with five bedrooms. Across the façade on the lakeside, buttresses are reintroduced and provide a graceful vertical rise. Little of Wright's interior designs remain after renovation. Planters, in horizontal board, span across the exterior and revive Wright's passion for inserting and lifting nature to the eye across the view. A large garage was later added in the same Prairie-design theme. This is the last of Wright's Lake Delavan houses. Of all his designs here, this is most reminiscent of his Prairie style so prevalent in Oak Park and River Forest. It is his most dramatic Wisconsin Prairie house outside of Taliesin. Summer cottages were a longtime Wright design product. Among his earliest structures were the cottages he designed for Louis Sullivan and James Charnley in 1890 at Ocean Springs, Mississippi. Among his other better-known summerhouses were those he designed for Thomas Gale in 1897 in the Upper Peninsula of Michigan. Wright's Lake Delavan houses still retain their character so deeply set in his Prairie synthesis. He achieved great size and proportion in each, relishing the rawness of nature that cradled his Forest homes.

GRAND BEACH, MICHIGAN

Grand Beach, Michigan, at the southern tip of Lake Michigan, has been a traditional enclave of the Chicago Irish for generations. An eighty-minute drive from Chicago, it's an easy ride for weekend jaunts and summer living. Some of Chicago's most well known political legends have made it their country retreat, not least of which are two generations of Chicago mayors, the late Richard J. Daley and his son Richard M. Daley. The earliest homes were simple beach cottages high atop the great sand dunes and expansive shoreline. Those modest structures now share the community with more elaborate homes, the product of large, fast Chicago grain and commodity fortunes. Just as America entered World War I, Frank Lloyd Wright designed three Prairie-style homes that remain the village's treasured jewels.

ERNEST VOSBURGH HOUSE

Address: 46208 Crescent Road, Grand Beach, Michigan

Built: 1916

Of the three homes designed by Frank Lloyd Wright in Grand Beach, Michigan, the Vosburgh House stands almost unblemished from its original form. Unlike the other two Wright structures in the village—the Joseph J. Bagley House and the W. S. Carr House (not shown)—this home is not located along the Lake Michigan shoreline, but rather set into the thick arbor of a rolling, natural forest, replete with a nearby creek. Such proximity to nature is a mark of Wright's personal aesthetic. Though the house is set back into the woods and entwines itself within the sandy landscape, it is close to neighbors and is a natural part of the neighborhood. The Vosburgh House's cruciform plan is familiar and its two-story living room is reminiscent of the Isabel Roberts House (1908) in River Forest and the Frank J. Baker House (1908) in Wilmette, which also features soaring, two-story glass window walls. The exterior stucco cladding with cedar and oak trim echoes the architectural voice of Wright's most familiar Prairie designs. The gentle, hipped roof has expansive overhangs that provide shelter and protection. The roof projections demonstrate an expansive sense of proportion and symmetry in this compact domestic dwelling. The central chimney is a special feature of Wright's Prairie design and the interior fireplace is fashioned in Norman brick, traditionally longer than common brick. This is a remarkably delightful house in a setting of strong natural sensitivities. The shadow of Wright is still unmistakably vibrant in this country Prairie cottage marked with enduring elegance and gentle style. Within the interior of the house, the living room sustains a small second-floor gallery balcony. Of all Wright's splendid Prairie houses, the Vosburgh House shoulders a unique refinement—a structure imbued with all the essential Prairie elements but without the bulk of more familiar dwellings. This is a hidden wonder on a modest scale. With the lake waters just a short walk away, this is the perfect beach house through the season. Every inch carries a unique architectural nobility, with Wright's aesthetic blending into nature.

Left: Wright designed three houses in Grand Beach, and only the Vosburgh House remains essentially as it was built. It is a Prairie gem of cruciform plan with a two-story-high living room.

INDEX